Frederick Augustus Mahan, Jean Baptiste Sébastien Krantz

**Study on reservoir walls**

Frederick Augustus Mahan, Jean Baptiste Sébastien Krantz

**Study on reservoir walls**

ISBN/EAN: 9783337717940

Printed in Europe, USA, Canada, Australia, Japan

Cover: Foto ©ninafisch / pixelio.de

More available books at **www.hansebooks.com**

# STUDY

ON

# RESERVOIR WALLS.

BY

J. B. KRANTZ,
INGÉNIEUR EN CHEF DES PONTS ET CHAUSSÉES.

*TRANSLATED FROM THE FRENCH*

BY

F. A. MAHAN,
CAPTAIN OF ENGINEERS, U. S. ARMY.

ILLUSTRATED BY 34 PLATES, COMPARING SECTIONS OF DAMS ACTUALLY
CONSTRUCTED WITH THE PROFILE-TYPES.

NEW YORK:
JOHN WILEY & SONS,
15 ASTOR PLACE.
1883.

50003

COPYRIGHT, 1883, BY
F. A. MAHAN.

PRESS OF J. J. LITTLE & CO.,
NOS. 10 TO 20 ASTOR PLACE, NEW YORK.

# AUTHOR'S PREFACE.

THE study now published was made during the year 1865. It bears the marks of the duties brought upon me by the service of the department of the Ardèche, of which I was then chief engineer.

Ordered to Paris, and placed successively in charge of a hard task at the Exposition and of an important navigation service, I laid my almost finished study aside up to the present time.

Since 1865 several articles have been written on the walls of reservoirs. I can especially mention the remarkable documents published in the *Annales des Ponts et Chaussées* (September and October, 1866) by MM. Graeff and Delocre.

I am certainly very well content to find that my views agree with those of the excellent engineers whose names I have just mentioned. Still I cannot but feel that their work takes away from mine, with its theoretical interest, a part of its practical usefulness. My first motion was, therefore, to shut it up in my drawer.

After some reflection I decided to publish it. In fact, it seems to me that this study, now shorn of all scientific appearance, and reduced to a sort of practical formulary, may still render to engineers the services that I expected from it myself at a certain time.

If this hope be realized, my object will be wholly accomplished.

J. B. KRANTZ.

PARIS, *January*, 17, 1870.

# TRANSLATOR'S PREFACE.

IN preparing this work for the American press, the translator has been guided by the same motive which led M. Krantz to publish it, viz : the hope that as a mere practical formulary, it might be of use to engineers whose duties lead them to the construction of reservoir walls.

Since M. Krantz wrote his work, M. Pelletreau has written a series of excellent articles in the following numbers of the *Annales des Ponts et Chaussées*: 1876, second half year ; 1877, second half year ; 1879, first half year. Those desiring to study this subject theoretically will do well to add these articles to those mentioned by M. Krantz.

As the mere transformation of the metric denominations into the English would cause the quantities in the drawings and tables to appear wholly arbitrary, I have thought it best to retain the metric values, while giving in all cases their English equivalents. On the drawings the English denominations are above the lines, and the metric below.

F. A. M.

DAVIS ISLAND DAM,
*August* 28, 1882.

# STUDY

## ON THE

# WALLS OF RESERVOIRS.

## I.

### GENERAL CONSIDERATIONS ON THE USEFULNESS OF TAKING GOOD CARE OF WATER.

AMONG the measures that may contribute to the increase of production, the complete husbanding of water has always been pointed out as one of the most effective.

In fact water gives at once a powerful stimulant to vegetation and a cheap motive power.

The influence of water on vegetation is too well known for it to be necessary to speak of it here. We need only say that but little land exists which may not become productive if watered; that there is no soil so fertile that its productiveness cannot be increased by irrigation. In short and in general terms we may say that scarcely any barren lands exist except those absolutely deprived of water, and that the maximum of production can only be obtained by watering.

In our day, the great industries use steam as the

motive power, it being produced by means of coal. But mineral fuel is not recreated.

The great reserves placed by nature at our disposal will certainly be sufficient for our generation and for those which immediately follow it. We may, however, foresee and even calculate the time when this precious resource will be wanting in Europe. On this account it must henceforth be economized either by better arrangements and a better control of our fires, or else by searching nature and utilizing the auxiliary forces which may, for certain purposes, replace steam.

Among these forces, the fall of water holds a prominent position on account of its economy and on account of the many cases in which it can be used to advantage.

The unceasing motion of aerial circulation is constantly raising and carrying immense quantities of water taken from the ocean and spreading them over the principal chains of mountains. Thence they return to the sea through various brooks and rivers to be again taken up and carried back. This incessant creation of force seems to be intimately connected with our planet and will only come to an end when it does. Wisely looked after, it will always be one of the most precious resources for industrial pursuits.

If water, as a motive power and as a stimulant for vegetation, have a preponderating part, its usefulness from another point of view is not less. It has become the basis of hygiene and domestic comfort, and every day larger supplies are called for in our cities.

The small ration of water that sufficed for our fathers is no longer enough for us. In vain is it largely increased; it is always less than the requirements of the people.

Needs of this kind have become so urgent that, in countries where the grouping of the population is not trammeled by old customs or by necessities of position, cities are seen to spring up at those points where large supplies of water satisfy new demands.

But if, from all these points of view, the wise caring for water becomes more and more desirable, it must also be noticed that it becomes more and more difficult.

As a consequence of very complex causes, of which the principal seem to be the cutting down of forests and the cultivation of the soil, the regimen of our streams is becoming more and more unsteady.

Dry, or very nearly so, in the summer, our rivers contain in the wet season large volumes of water. If their slope be great, they become real torrents which scatter ruin and desolation along their banks.

The small summer discharge does not at all show a lack of volume in the water that falls. Far from it. The department of the Ardèche, toward which my thoughts turn while writing these lines, is one of those in which this giving out of the springs in summer is most remarkable, and still it is of all the departments of France the most widely endowed with rains. The high chains of the Tanargue, the Coyrons and the Mézen stop, chill and condense the winds saturated with moisture from the Mediterranean, and force them to pour out great masses of water on the ground.

Observations made at Mézillac, in the midst of the Coyrons chain, and at Montpezat, show a mean annual rainfall of 1 m. 91 (75.6 inches). At Joyeuse, on November 9, 1827, the rain that fell during 21 hours reached the enormous height of, 0 m. 729 (28.7 inches).

The quanity of rain that falls in the Ardèche is therefore very great, but on the other hand it is very unequally distributed over the different parts of the year. The same may be said of many of the departments of the south of France and of Algiers.

This unequal distribution of rain causes two terrible scourges—floods and prolonged droughts. The former scatters more ruin in a short time and strikes the minds of the people more than the other. The second, less destructive in appearance, covers a greater extent of territory and really does much more harm.

A remedy has long been sought for these natural scourges, and it has been thought to be found in the construction of vast stores of water which will substitute a rational husbanding for the capricious and often ill-regulated supplies brought by atmospheric agents.

It is not uninteresting to see within what limits, on this point, man may, with the resources furnished by his own industry, overcome the infirmities of his condition.

There can be no doubt of this so far as droughts are concerned. The stores that place at the disposal of agriculture and industry, for use during dry spells, the surplus put away during the rainy season, correct very effectively the inequality in nature's supplies.

This is manifest in principle, and, moreover, experience has shown that this remedy is in so far very effective that the water thus stored does not cost more than agriculture and industry can afford to pay.

From the earliest times there have been built, in India and Ceylon, reservoirs which have called forth about them real oases of greenness and fertility.

Wherever, by reason of the frequent revolutions of the East, these useful monuments, the fruits of peace and the legacy of a provident administration, were destroyed or perished through want of being kept in repair, the rich cultivation which their existence called forth disappeared with them. Jungles and banks of sand took possession of the ground only to disappear again when the reservoirs were rebuilt.

Demonstration on this point is complete, and the splendid works for storing water and for irrigation executed in the south of Spain, furnish an example nearer to our doors but not more conclusive as to the effectiveness of reservoirs against long continued droughts.

In his very remarkable study on the floods of the Loire, M. Comoy shows that the height, and consequently the destructive effects of floods can be much lessened by building in the upper parts of the valleys of the Loire and the Allier 85 reservoirs, having a total capacity of 592 millions of cubic metres (20,904 millions of cubic feet).

It is difficult to doubt the justice of M. Comoy's observations and the exactness of the consequences that he deduces therefrom. Still, at bottom, all this ingenious system rests on a sort of control that the reservoirs must establish by delaying the arrival, at certain points, of the rises of some of the tributaries. But this presupposes a very nearly established order in the times of the rises of these tributaries, and, consequently, of the atmospheric phenomena which cause them. Now this order cannot be absolute. Nothing proves that it may not be changed or even inverted, whence it follows that the delay in some streams may cause troublesome coincidences of the maxima of rises, and aggravate in some part of the river the destructive effects which it was thought to lessen.

Assuming even that the spontaneous working of the projected reservoirs will always exert the moderating action expected from them, it may be asked whether the capital engaged in these colossal structures might not be differently and more efficaciously used. Might not the interest be more simply divided among the riparian owners who are reached by the floods? Better still, would it not answer to keep up, with this interest and the insurance premiums voluntarily payed in by the riparian owners themselves, a large mutual-assistance fund? The disasters caused by floods, which after all only come at long intervals, would in this way be probably sufficiently covered.

I am free to confess that this system of cure substituted for the one proposed is less flattering to human pride; but, after all, what does it matter if the result sought be brought about without too many sacrifices! So long as the remedy is effective, and as it properly repairs the damages done by the flood, we need not be too particular about inquiring whether it comes from the methods of economists or from the art of the engineer.

Assuming that the system so carefully studied by M. Comoy be fully effective on the Loire; assuming, moreover, that it be not better to substitute a system of mutual insurance, we may still be allowed to ask whether the same methods will everywhere produce the same results. This may be doubted, and, for my part, certain facts, such as the one I am going to mention, do not give me much confidence on this point.

The dams projected for the valley of the Ardèche, to prevent the return of the great floods of this river, gave a total capacity of 60 millions of cubic metres (212 millions of cubic feet). To build them would have required great amounts of money, and the taking possession of large tracts of fertile land in a country which possesses but little. More could scarcely be done, and still it was, as will be seen, wholly insufficient.*

The River Ardèche discharged from midnight of September 9th, 1857, to noon of the next day, 86,400,000 cubic metres (305 millions of cubic feet), and in

---

* See the article by M. Marchegay in the *Annales*, 1861, 1st half year, pp. 1 to 16.

the succeeding 22 hours there was a further discharge of 351,936,000 cubic metres (12,427,860,000 cubic feet.)

Assuming all the reservoirs to have been absolutely empty on the morning of September 8th, they would have been filled during the 8th and 9th, and from the 10th would have ceased to act.

The rise of September 9th would have been lessened; that of the 10th, which was very destructive, would have preserved all its frightful violence.

It is true that M. Comoy assigns to his reservoirs a more complex task than that of mere storage. He assumes that when open at the gorge they discharge water while they still receive it, and, from the beginning, only hold a part of what comes into them. In this way they give up during the falling period of the flood the water accumulated during the rise. But in the present case, this ingenious working would have been of little avail. The reservoirs would have been half filled during the 9th, and would only have been able to withdraw from the discharge of the 10th about 30 millions of cubic metres (106 millions of cubic feet), which would not have been enough to sensibly change the height of the water and the damages caused thereby.

Hence it would be imprudent, in my opinion, to assume at present that we possess any preventive which can be generally used, and which is certainly effective against the scourge of inundations. This scourge often, if not always, exceeds our knowledge and resources.

This is not the case with prolonged droughts. Wherever they occur, so long as it does not arise from a radical insufficiency in the amount of rain annually poured upon the ground, but from excessive irregularity in its distribution, the remedy has long been found, and we may wonder that it has not been oftener used.

In fact, it is enough to store up the excess of water that falls during the wet season, and to keep it for the dry.

This storing up is one of the most useful and industrially productive operations that can be performed.

I have already said this before, but a few facts and figures, taken from the department of the Ardèche, allow me to make myself more clear on this point.

Sloping to the Rhone on the east, the department of the Ardèche rests on the west against the hills of the Cevennes and the last abutments of the Auvergne. It is like a gigantic inclined plane, of which the lower edge is formed by the Rhone at about 85 metres (279 feet) above the level of the sea, and of which the upper edge reaches altitudes of 1,200, 1,400, and even 1,750 metres (3,900, 4,600, and 6,750 feet), at Mézen above the same level. The width of the inclined plane is about 60 kilometres (nearly 40 miles).

In rolling from these heights to the Rhone this water develops a very considerable motive power, which is already utilized, but from which greater service might be obtained.

If the fall of the water be limited to 1,000 metres (3,300 feet), we find that not more than 2,400 cubic metres (8,500 cubic feet) of water are required to create in the fall the same work that a one-horse-power engine could produce, if in constant operation during the entire year. In this proportion, the construction of a reservoir having a capacity of 2,400,000 cubic metres (85,000,000 cubic feet) at the top of the mountain is equivalent to creating a force of a 1,000 horse-power engine.

Figuring out all the expenses, we find that, under ordinary circumstances, a cubic metre of water stored in the reservoirs cost about 0.015f. ($0.000083 per cubic foot). This supposes that the reservoir is only filled once a year; if it be filled twice, the cost is reduced to 0.0075f. ($0.000042 per cubic foot); it may even come as low as 0.005f. ($0.000027 per cubic foot) if it be filled three times. With the quantity of rain that habitually falls on the high mountains of the Ardèche, two and three fillings a year may frequently be had; but counting only on one, the gross cost per horse-power only reaches 36 francs ($7.20) per year, which is certainly not dear.

If it be added that this water, filtered over beds of basalt or granite, is generally extremely pure, and thoroughly fit for currying leather, dyeing wools, bleaching linen and paper, the great industrial interest attaching to its use will have been pointed out.

Considerations of another kind, taken in the same localities, show that this good care of water, everywhere so desirable, may sometimes become a necessity of the highest order.

In 1864 the department of the Ardèche contained 1,440 hydraulic works, used, in general, for milling and for spinning of silks. Few in number and very small in the beginning, these establishments have multiplied out of proportion on some streams, and in perfecting their plant have needed a greater motive power—that is, a greater supply of water.

During three-quarters of the year the water is sufficient for the factories, and the owners live in peace. But when the summer sets in, the rivers only contain a thin stream of water in the midst of a wide bed. Penury begins, and with it come fierce competition and lawsuits before all the courts.

Armed with their laws and regulations, the courts intervene, but almost always without success. Whatever firmness they display, with whatever sagacity they apply the salutary prescriptions of the law, the struggle and anarchy hold on. The force of circumstances carries away both the careful equity of the judges and the real good will of the people themselves. It would be difficult to tell the amount of strength, intelligence, work and money spent in these constantly renewed struggles, and the unceasing trouble that they bring about in the relations of the inhabitants.

Taking care properly of the water, by keeping for the summer a part of the winter's surplus, would do more to pacify interests, to set at rest internal discords, than the wisest rules, how carefully soever they be applied.

*Pisciculture.*—In the Ardèche, as elsewhere, much attention is given to pisciculture. This attention is the more legitimate, as the rivers of this department seem to be well adapted to rearing fish, and contain some excellent kinds.

But when summer comes, all these fishes are obliged to take refuge in holes where a little water still remains. They there develop poorly, being too much confined, and become an easy prey to all marauders.

The temptation is such that all contrivances, whether permitted or not, all methods, *even poisoning*, are used to destroy them, and at the end of each summer they have almost entirely disappeared.

By keeping a little water in the rivers during the dry season, an end would be put to this unintelligent destruction.

Thus, from whatever point of view we look at it, the proper caring for water appears as one of the most useful works that can be done. It is not rash to think that when the needs for roadways shall have ceased to be urgent, which cannot be far away, public attention will be turned in this direction.

Is it necessary to say it? Water can only be properly stored by means of deep ponds set in the upper parts of valleys. There is found, as a rule, the greatest facility for building the dams of reservoirs. It is there, also, that the stored-up water may do the most good, since, in coming down, it is found at all stages, either as a motive power or as an irrigator.

The preceding considerations will doubtless appear somewhat ambitious as a preamble to a note intended to set forth the best shape to be given to reservoir walls.

Still, as these are the considerations which led me to the study which I now give to the public, I thought that they might also be of some interest to the reader, and assist him in enduring the dry examination of the technical considerations which are to follow.

## II.

### RESERVOIR WALLS.

*Glance at the walls of existing dams.*—At first attributed to the Moors, whose solicitude for agricultural works, and consequently for the good care of water, is well known, the great reservoirs of the south of Spain seem to be a decidedly Spanish creation.

It is a glorious token, which Spain can lay claim to with just pride, because these immense works show a great persistence of views and a marked appreciation of the real conditions of richness for a country in the people who paid for them out of their savings, and who resorted, in order to build them, to the powerful lever of association.

The kings of Spain themselves, taken up as they were with their external struggles and with their conquests in two worlds, not only placed no obstacles in the way of these great works of peace, but even gave them great encouragement. They should be equally praised.

Here eulogy must necessarily stop, because the execution of the walls of the dams was not equal to the high economic conceptions that gave birth to the projects.

In fact, it is easy to see, in the great size and immense extent of the masses employed, a complete lack of understanding of the intensity and distribution of the forces to be overcome. Not knowing how to find the direction of these forces, or to calculate their intensities exactly, they doubled or trebled the necessary volumes of masonry, and, instead of the graceful and elegant structures at which we have now arrived, they built prodigious walls that excite astonishment, and show a small amount of skill combined with an immense energy of will.

The figures accompanying this note show that,

however sharp it may be, this criticism is not too severe, and that if the walls of the Spanish reservoirs are respectable through their age, imposing through their mass, they still belong, in reality, to the infancy of art. It is in vain that, with unthinking enthusiasm, it has been desired to call the great wall of Alicante, the principal one among them, by the name of Herrera; the name of the illustrious architect of the Escorial has nothing to gain by this tardy recognition.

More soberly conceived, more wisely built, the reservoir walls constructed in France for the water supply of the canals have not the imposing air of the Spanish works, but they show a clearer conception of the forces to be overcome and greater care in regard to economy. In a word, they show a real advance in the art of building.

Still they are not irreproachable—far from it. Among those which I might mention is the Gros-Bois wall (Fig. 30) for example, which, now not very strong, would very nearly satisfy all conditions of stability if it were turned around; that is, if the upstream side were down-stream and the reverse.

A new era for the construction of reservoir walls dates from the article published by Sazilly in the *Annales des Ponts et Chaussées* (1853, 2d half year). With rare insight, Sazilly was able to discern the nature, amount and direction of the various forces which act on reservoir walls at the different periods of filling the basins. From them he deduces rational forms to be given to constructions of this sort.

I take the liberty of not wholly sharing Sazilly's opinion and of saying that his profiles leave something to be desired. But I cannot speak too highly of the esteem in which I hold his excellent work. Furthermore, the engineers of the Ponts et Chaussées, who, since that time, have had to construct reservoir walls have been evidently inspired by Sazilly's ideas. It is easy to see this in the very correct profiles of the wall of Ternay, the Furens and the Habra, which leave far behind them any previously built.

Taking up the subject where Sazilly left it, MM. Graeff and Delocre published in the *Annales des Ponts et Chaussées* (September and October, 1866) two very good articles which, in my opinion, leave nothing to be desired.*

The theoretical study of reservoir walls may therefore be regarded as definitely fixed except in some points of detail. Constructors have now little to do but follow the track so clearly marked out.

*Choice of the system of dam.*—Three principal systems have been used in building dams of large reservoirs: viz., earthen embankments, masonry walls and walls and embankments together.

This last system has rarely been successful. It has

---

* See also articles by M. Pelletreau in the *Annales* for 1876, 1877, 1879. —[TR.]

all the defects of both the others and seems to be much the most expensive. I therefore mention it only to call it to mind.

Built principally in England, Scotland and the centre of France, earthen dams seem to be most useful when the ground is not adapted for the foundations of walls. They work better in mild, damp climates than in dry and warm where the earth of which they are made is apt to crack and form fissures; but deep ponds cannot be made with them without great cost.

In fact, the volume of earth to be used increases rapidly when the height increases; and, as the embankments must be made with extreme care and with selected earth, it does not appear that there is any advantage in building earthen dams beyond a height of 30 metres (100 feet).

Climatic conditions, the nature of the ground, the facilities which it offers for the construction of masonry, have generally given the preference to walls over earthen dams in Spain and the south of France. More easily and quickly built, soon water-tight, free from settling, the wall deserves the preference, especially for great heights, provided always that the ground admits of its being firmly founded.

Moreover, it is easy to see that the costs of these two styles of constructions do not differ so much as would appear at first glance.

Embankments should always be made of carefully selected earth, sufficient but not too much clay and sandy, but not in excess. It should be carefully cleansed, before use, of pebbles, roots and easily decomposed bodies.

Finally, it should be carefully laid in successive layers of 0.10 m. (4 inches), in thickness, well rammed, or better still, compressed with grooved rollers. Moreover, it must be protected on the side of the water by means of some sort of stone work to prevent the waves from injuring the slopes of the dam. Whence it follows that, in spite of the coarseness of the materials used, earthen dams cannot but be costly.

In respect to economy they do not therefore offer any special advantages over masonry walls.

If we compare earthen dams sustaining a pond 30 metres (100 feet) deep with masonry walls of the same height, we find that the wall requires 332 cubic metres of masonry per running metre (132 cubic yards per running foot), which at $4.00 per cubic metre for everything, including the facing, gives $1,328.

With its slopes of 1 perpendicular to 2 base, its crown set at 3 metres (10 feet) above the level of the water, and with a dry stone paving on the up-stream side, the earthen dam would cost per running metre:

3062 cubic yards of embankment @ $0.37. . . . . . . $1133.05
96.46 " " " dry stone pavement @ $0.75 . . . $72.34

Total. . . . . . . . . . . . . . . . . . . . . . . . $1,205.39

which is very nearly the same price as the wall. The difference even disappears if we consider the interest on the capital engaged during construction and the long repairs that are sometimes required by large embankments on account of the settling of the earth.

Viewing the question from all sides, it seems to me that there is a real advantage in building reservoir dams of masonry, whenever the ground shows, at a reasonable depth, sufficiently firm strata on which to build, and it is only when proper bottom cannot be found that recourse should be had to earthen dams.

It seems to me, then, that masonry dams should be the rule and the others the exception, especially for great heights.

*Kind of masonry to be used.*—The dimensions and shapes for the walls of reservoirs depend, it can easily be understood, on the strength of the material used. It is therefore interesting to examine what kinds of masonry should be put into them.

The Spanish engineers, in these sorts of structures, as well as in the others, used immense amounts of cut stone. This choice seems to have been brought about by the abundance of quarries over a great part of their territory, and also by certain habits of size and majesty inherent in their character.

The French engineers, yielding to other considerations and following other customs, have, especially in later times, used more common materials. Which were right, the French or the Spanish? This is what we must examine.

Under ordinary circumstances, masonry of rough random stone, set firmly in good hydraulic mortar, does not cost, all facing included, more than $4 per cubic metre ($3.05 per cubic yard). Cut stone as a general rule costs three or four times as much and can sustain but little more than double the load. Whence it follows that it is better, as regards economy, to make a surface of a given strength with rough masonry rather than with cut-stone.

In the present case the preference has also another cause. The external forces that a reservoir wall resists have directions which depend upon the shape of the inner face and which, as a rule, are but slightly inclined to the horizon. Hence it is necessary to give a certain width to the base, otherwise the resultant of the thrusts and pressures might pass outside. It is therefore evident that if we wished, in order to reduce the width of the base, to utilize the full strength of the stone, it could only be done within very narrow limits, which would not by any means make up the difference in the cost of the materials.

For economical reasons as well as for facility in building, it seems to me certain that rubble masonry is what should be used. The joints should be irregular on the faces and in all the sections; the courses should be thoroughly inter-locked, or better still there should be no courses, and by means of good work this result must be obtained, so that the whole body of the wall shall be a real monolith.

Rubble masonry has also this advantage that it adapts itself without any special stones to every possible sort of shape. The most complex curves require no other care than to define them by means of suitably placed templets on which the mason directs his work. This advantage is also not to be overlooked.

*Weight of a cubic yard of masonry.*—The weight of a cubic yard of well-built masonry of hard stone, granite or limestone, may be set at 3,900 pounds and is thus determined :

| | |
|---|---|
| For an actual volume of 0.67 of stone at 4,250 pounds per cubic yard.... ................. | 2,847 lbs. |
| For an actual volume of 0.33 of mortar at 3,230 pounds per cubic yard..................... | 1,077 lbs. |
| which makes in all............. | 3,924 lbs. |

Or in round numbers 3,900 pounds (2,300 kilograms per cubic metre).

By adopting almost everywhere the figure of 3,400 pounds (2,000 kilograms per cubic metre), more convenient it is true in calculations, engineers seem to me to have unduly lightened the true weight of the structure.

*Limit of the strain to be put upon the masonry.*—It being granted that reservoir walls should be built of hard rubble masonry, well made with hydraulic mortar, I think that they should never be called upon to sustain a greater strain than 6 kilograms per square centimetre (85 pounds per square inch).

Certainly, under ordinary circumstances, well built masonry of this kind should sustain a much greater weight.

But we must remark that the formulæ by means of which we determine the decomposition and transmission of the forces acting on large reservoir walls, are only founded on hypotheses which it is impossible to verify exactly. Hence we obtain probable results, but absolute certainty is wanting, and consequently we must be prudent.

And, as a matter of fact, the upper parts of dams must resist the action of waves and ice, and may, in heavy squalls, receive violent shocks. On the other hand, there may be added to the pressure of the water at the lower part, the pressure of a thick deposit of mud, which greatly increases the transverse strains. These circumstances must be taken into consideration.

If, by adopting a maximum resistance of 8 kilograms per square centimetre (115 pounds per square inch) instead of 6, the volume of the masonry used would be reduced in proportion of 6 to 8, the interest attaching to a complete utilization of the strength of the masonry might be understood; but such is not the case. For such an overcharge the saving in volume is not much, and, when everything is taken into account, we should be exposed, without special advantages, to very great risk.

For it must always be borne in mind that of all hydraulic structures, the reservoir wall is perhaps the most difficult to properly repair after it has once been seriously damaged. It is also the one which causes the most disastrous consequences if once it gives way.

The breaking of the Puentes dam on the 30th of April, 1802, caused the loss of 608 persons and destroyed the little town of Lorea containing 809 houses.

The rupture of the Sheffield dam also caused the deaths of many persons and the ruins of many structures.

In view of such chances, the engineer must not be too bold, nor take upon himself, before the public, a responsibility which is powerless to repair such disasters.

However little it may lean toward rashness, boldness, in such a case, may become almost a crime. It should be severely proscribed and the rule of strict prudence should always be followed. In my opinion, it is better not to build reservoir walls if we have not the necessary resources to build solidly, than to build *carelessly* and at the risk of frightful catastrophes.

On all these accounts I think that in calculating strength, the pressure of 6 kilograms per square centimetre (85 pounds per square inch) should never be overstepped.

*Considerations on the shape to be given to reservoir walls.*—I have said before that rubble masonry is better than any other for building reservoir walls, because with it we can follow any shape without having the trouble of cutting any special stones, and consequently we are left free to choose that shape of profile which will offer the greatest amount of strength.

I have also said that it is prudent not to exceed a pressure of 6 kilograms per square centimetre (85 pounds per square inch) of surface, and finally that we are about right in taking the weight of the masonry at 2,300 kilograms per cubic metre (3,900 pounds per cubic yard).

This granted, the data essential to determining the shape of the profile are given and we can proceed to the calculations. Still it is not uninteresting to examine another accessory arrangement, very frequently adopted in Spain but generally neglected in France. I mean the shape of the wall, curved in plan with its convex side up-stream. At the first glance we see that this curve must transfer a part of the pressures to the sides of the valley, and that the wall, under the action of the heads of water, closing tighter against the solid banks that hold it, has no tendency to turn over.

A short but sufficiently accurate calculation shows this first impression to be right.

If, in a curved reservoir wall, we take a horizontal section at a depth $h$ below the level of the water, if we

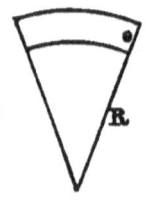

call $e$ the uniform thickness of the wall of the section under consideration, $R$ the mean radius of curvature, $w$ the weight of the unit of the liquid and $w'$ the mean load on the thickness $e$, we may, with a certain degree of exactness, establish the following relation between these different quantities:

$$w h R = w' e.$$

If we now make $w = 1{,}000$ kilograms per cubic metre (62.5 pounds per cubic foot), $w' = 60{,}000$ kilograms per square metre (12,240 pounds per square foot), $e = \frac{1}{3} h$, we shall find $R = 20$ metres (65 feet.)

Which means that under the above conditions we may, by laying out the wall on a curve of 20 metres (65 feet) radius, transfer the pressure of the water to the sides of the valley, which will thus act as abutments, and that, too, no matter what the height. But, on the other hand, this arrangement in a curve does not at all lessen the effect of the weight of the masonry, which, acting perpendicularly to the plane of the section considered, cannot be transmitted to the end. Hence it follows that whether the structure be curved or not, its weight must always be supported in the same way. The saving that follows the adoption of a curved shape has a bearing only on the increase that must be given to a wall which already supports its own weight, in order to make it support, at the same time, the pressure of the water.

This reduces by a large amount the profit derived from adopting a curved form; still, though thus limited, the advantage is real, and we cannot afford to set it aside wherever the locality will allow its use. But it will be prudent not to consider it in making our calculations for stability. The result of this voluntary omission will be to obtain in the structure an excess of strength which is never to be despised.

In France and elsewhere, reservoir walls have frequently been reinforced by means of counterforts. The usefulness of this device is, in my opinion, very doubtful. If the wall is strong enough by itself, it is clear that the counterforts are a useless expense as well as a complication in the system of construction.

If the wall is not sufficiently strong, the counterforts will not prevent it from yielding under the pressure as may be seen in the Lampy and Grosbois reservoirs.

In a word, the masonry intended for the counterforts will always be better used if it be spread over the wall than if it be used by itself under the shape of pillars or projecting masses.

This being said, counterforts suppressed, curvature admitted as an excess of strength, what should be the profile of the wall?

In order to determine it, we need consider but one element of the wall included between two adjacent vertical planes perpendicular to the face of the wall, then arrange it so that it will resist by itself the loads and pressures put upon it. And in fact, it is clear that if each of these elements, taken by itself, be sufficiently strong, its connection with the adjoining elements and with the sides of the valley can only increase the stability of the whole.

The question then resolves itself into making one

element stable, and for this two situations are to be considered, which are the extreme terms of the successive situations through which the wall passes, when the reservoir being empty it is filled to its highest point, or being entirely full it is reduced to complete emptiness. In a word, the wall must be wholly stable before the pond exists and after it is complete. Stability, being established for these two extreme cases, must exist in all the intermediate positions, about which we need give ourselves no concern.

When the reservoir is empty, the wall only supports its own weight, but even then the base carries a heavy load. Thus it is easy to see that if the wall has a uniform thickness, it cannot be more than 26 metres (85.3 feet) high before the pressure on the base exceeds 6 kilograms per square centimetre (85 pounds per square inch). If the faces be inclined so as to reduce the mean thickness to one-half and then to one-third of the width of the base, the height compatible with a pressure of 6 kilograms rises to 52 metres (170.6 feet), then to 78 metres (255.9 feet).

This simple consideration shows that it is absolutely necessary to widen the base of the walls by inclining the up and down-stream faces. If the wall were not exposed to a heavy pressure on its up-stream face the bâtirs on the two faces would be the same, and, by this fact of complete symmetry, the pressures would be uniformly distributed.

But when the water is in and the reservoir is full,

the water bears upon the up-stream face of the wall and there develops a pressure which increases with the square of the depth of the water. In deep reservoirs this pressure becomes enormous. Made up of elements normal to the face of the wall, it exerts its final effect in a nearly horizontal direction and carries the maximum load to the back of the wall. The weight, however, not ceasing to act, these two forces have a resultant which must, for stability, pierce the base in front of the back edge. Hence arises the necessity of giving to the down-stream face a greater bâtir than to the up-stream.

I have taken for the up-stream bâtir the fixed ratio of five perpendicular to one base. For the down-stream face the ratio is not fixed but increases with the height. To justify this arrangement it will be sufficient to turn to tables II*a* and II*b*, and see that the pressures increase regularly and that they nowhere exceed the limits adopted.

To sum up, the wall of a reservoir must have somewhat the same silhouette as a wrestler who is ready to receive a shock, and who, well set on his legs, has carried one a little forward while the other is strongly planted behind.

*Width at the top.*—Theoretically the width of the wall at the top might be nothing, since at this point there is neither a pressure of water, nor any weight of masonry. But in practice we must consider the shock of waves and ice which may, in certain cases, acquire great strength and exert a powerful destroying action at the top.

The wall also should be made use of to form a means of communication between the two slopes of the valley. The interest in thus using the wall as a viaduct is the greater in proportion as the pond is deeper, and, consequently, as the lake artificially formed extends further and forms a greater obstacle to communication.

Without having any absolute connection with the depth of the pond, the width of the crown depends upon it to a certain extent, and we easily see that it must increase at the same time. It seems to me scarcely possible to reduce it below 2 metres (6.56 feet) for small ponds, nor necessary to make it more than 5 metres (16.40 feet) for the largest. I think it should be kept within these limits.

*Height of the crown.*—M. Minard mentions, in his *Cours de construction*, waves which rose 3 metres (9.84 feet) above the water level in the Chazilly reservoir, the pond being but 1,500 metres (4,900 feet) long and 20 metres (66 feet) deep.

Waves have reached the height of 2 metres (6.56 feet) in the Cercey reservoir, the greatest length of which is 900 metres (2,950 feet), and depth 10 metres (33 feet).

The size of waves depends upon very complex

causes, among which may be mentioned the force and direction of the wind, the length of the pond and the depth of the water; but it is difficult, if not impossible, to establish any exact relation between the phenomenon and its different causes—in other words, to fix in advance the height that the waves will reach in any given case.

Having a certain number of observations as a basis, I think that the height of the crown should increase with the depth of the water, and I have set 3.50 metres (11.50 feet) as a maximum, not including the parapet. Still, if there were any occasion for changing the figures given in column 4, tables I*a* and I*b*, it should be, in my opinion, rather by increasing than diminishing them. In fact, it is hard to see that there would be any serious disadvantage in having the crown a metre (3.28 feet) too high. But there would be a great inconvenience in having it a metre too low, especially were the wall to be used as a viaduct.

*Justification of the types.*—The object of the preceding considerations is to state the problem distinctly, and to clearly define the conditions that the wall must fulfill.

This done, in order to find the solution, we only have to resort to the strict formulæ of analysis, and to establish an exact connection between the various variables, of which the relations have been pointed out in a general way. But, on this point, I can do neither better nor more than those who have gone before me, nor can I say anything that has not already been set forth with so much authority by Sazilly first and afterwards by Delocre (and again by Pelletreau. Tr.) For the theoretical study of the subject I shall therefore limit myself to referring to the excellent articles which I have mentioned, and approaching the problem by another road, I shall justify, *a posteriori*, my profile-type by showing that it fulfills in all respects the various conditions that we have sought to obtain.

*Sliding on the base or on the courses.*—A reservoir wall is necessarily founded on a bed of firm rock. The defective parts must be cleared away, and the rock cut into steps rising from the up- to the downstream side, or, more simply still, irregularly cut down, with projections left here and there in the sound parts of the mass.

I have said before that the masonry should be rubble, without any regular beds, so built as to form a true monolith.

Under these conditions sliding is impossible, either of the wall on its foundation, or of one bed on another.

Still, it is not uninteresting to inquire what would happen to the proposed profile, if these precautions were not taken.

Now, we know that the force required to make two pieces of cut stone slide upon each other, when both are dry, or when they are joined by fresh mortar, is equal to about 0.75 of the normal pressure. Whence it follows that the sliding of our walls would only be possible when the horizontal thrust reached three-fourths of the sum of the vertical pressures. If we consult line 17, of tables II*a* and II*b*, we find that the ratio of the thrust to the pressure varies from 0.34 to 0.51.

With these conditions, and even more so when the foundation bed shall have been cut down with the care that should be taken to make it rough and lumpy, there would be no tendency to slide.

*Tendency to overturn.*—Made with good hydraulic mortar, masonry has a great deal of cohesion and adheres strongly to the rock, whence it follows that it can resist the considerable forces of traction, which should be considered in calculating the resistance against overturning. But, to simplify the problem, I shall suppose that the wall does not adhere to its bed, and that the condition to be fulfilled to prevent overturning is, that the moment of the thrust shall be less than the moment of the vertical pressures, distances being measured with regard to the down-stream edge. Now, line 16, tables II*a* and II*b*, shows us that the ratio between these two moments varies from 0.19 to 0.40. Hence there is perfect stability in this respect, without even considering the force of cohesion, which is still real.

*Pressures on the base.*—When the resultant of the pressures pierces the base at an equal distance from the two outside edges, there is no reason why these two edges should be unequally loaded. We assume, and we must assume, that they are equally so. But if the resultant approach one edge the equality ceases, and the nearer edge to the point of application of the resultant supports a greater share of the load. I have adopted for the determination of the pressures the following usual rule:

$l$ being the width of the wall, $R$ the resultant of the pressures, $u$ the distance of the point of application of this resultant from the nearer edge, and $P$ the maximum pressure, we have

$$P = \frac{2}{3}\frac{R}{u}; \text{ or } P = \frac{2R}{l}\left(2 - \frac{3u}{l}\right),$$

according as $u$ is less or greater than $\frac{l}{3}$.

This granted, when the pool is empty, all the forces are summed up in a weight which is nearer the front edge than the other; hence it is on the front edge that the maximum pressure is found. Calculated according to the preceding rule, it never exceeds 5.97, say 6 kilograms per square centimetre (85 pounds per square inch).

The average pressure, supposing it to be uniformly distributed over the entire base, nowhere exceeds 4.55 kilograms (64.70 pounds).

The ratio of the second to the first never falls below 0.62, which shows a good distribution of the forces.

When the pool is full, the resultant of the forces is no longer vertical. If it be decomposed at its point of application into two components, one parallel and the other normal to the base, we find that the horizontal component, which is but the thrust of the water on the vertical projection of the wall, is powerless to cause any sliding on the base. Moreover, on account of its direction, it does not aid in increasing the load which remains due to the vertical component. The point of application of the resultant being nearer to the down-stream edge than to the other, it is the down-stream edge that sustains the maximum pressure. In no type does it exceed 5.71 kilograms per square centimetre (81.20 pounds per square inch). Uniformly distributed it reaches 5.65 kilograms (80.24 pounds).

The ratio of the mean to the maximum pressure varies from 0.50 to 0.98. But for the great heights it approaches unity, a result we should try to obtain.

*Expenses compared.*—In what precedes I have tried to show that the types are sound, so far as stability is concerned. I have shown that they are secure against sliding, overturning, and, finally, whether the pond be full or empty, there is no load on them which at any point exceeds 6 kilograms per square centimetre (85 pounds per square inch).

Undoubtedly, when we think on the one hand of the difficulty of making extensive repairs in reservoir walls, and on the other of the frightful disasters which their giving way may involve, we are led to consider perfect stability as the first condition to be fulfilled. This goes far beyond all the others, and there must be no doubt whatever as to the solidity of the wall.

But this condition being fulfilled, we may examine the question of cost, because these kinds of works, always very expensive, may, if they be badly designed, cause the locking up of a great deal of capital. We must therefore examine, on the score of economy, the value of the types which I offer.

The best means of justifying these types is to compare them with already existing similar works.

This comparison has no bearing except on the quantities of masonry which both require, because we must suppose that the masonry will be everywhere built in the same way, and always very simply.

The comparison of volumes manifestly becomes that of the surfaces of sections, and consequently can readily be made clear to the eye.

In figures 21, 22 and following, 14 specimens are thus compared with the types, and it is the result of this comparison which I am about to examine.

*Walls of Spanish reservoirs.*—The group of Spanish walls is first presented, with their imposing and useless size (figs. 22, 23, 24, 25, 28 and 29).

I attach so high an importance to perfect safety that I should feel very indulgent for this immoderate luxury if, in doubling the volume of the masonry, they had at the same time reduced the pressures to a large extent. Unfortunately, not this but the reverse is the case. Thus, for example, in the Elcho and Alicante dams the maximum pressures reach 12.70 kilograms and 11.30 kilograms per square centimetre (200.59 lbs. and 160.69 lbs. per square inch) respectively. It is nearly the same thing with the others.

The superiority of our later French types, so sober and so correct, over the cyclopean types of the Spanish walls, cannot for an instant be doubted.

*Old walls of French reservoirs.*—The French walls existing before Sazilly's article also form an interesting class to examine. This is the object of figs. 30, 31, 32, 33 and 34.

In these there is no longer cause for reproach in the dangerous luxury of masonry. Still there is considerable but at the same time much less excess.

All these examples, however, contain markedly more masonry than the new types, and err in regard to economy; but this is not the strongest reproach which a judicious criticism might most justly cast upon them.

By examining them closely, we easily see the uncertainty that then existed in the minds of engineers on the nature of the forces to be overcome. For example, in the Gros-Bois and Glomel walls almost all the surplus thickness is placed on the up-stream side. The contrary is the case in the Bosméléa wall.

That of Vioreau is a sort of rectangle with nearly vertical faces. At Lampy, the projections are marked, but they are about equal on the two sides.

All the profiles are incorrect, and the very diversities of their defects clearly show the absence of any sound theory.

*New French walls.*—The group of new French walls, represented by those of the Habra (fig. 27), of Térnay (fig. 26) and of the Furens (fig. 21), appears with an air of close relationship and an undoubted superiority. We easily see that they proceed from the same order of ideas and that the theory of walls is made and accepted by engineers.

Here the comparison becomes more serious.

WALL OF THE HABRA.

It is clear, at the first glance, that the type proposed requires about the same quantity of masonry as that of the Habra. In regard to economy there is very little to choose between them.

But the superiority from this point of view would belong to the profile-type if that, which I cannot but regard as a mistake in the shape of the parapet of the other, were corrected. It seems to me certain that if the wind were to raise waves in the pond, they would pass over the parapet, and might even upset it. This is a fault of inadvertence which should be corrected, and if what is necessary in this respect be done, our profile-type will show a slight saving on the other.

### WALL OF TERNAY.

The profile-type, as may be seen in fig. 26, has a little more of a bâtir up-stream than the Ternay wall. On the other hand it has a little less masonry down-stream. On the whole the two balance each other.

The reservoir wall of Ternay, which was remarkably planned and built by M. Bouvier, has, in my opinion, scarcely a defect. The up-stream face is a little too stiff. The pressure when empty is thereby increased and certainly exceeds 6 kilograms per square centimetre (85 pounds per square inch).

### WALL OF THE FURENS.

The reservoir wall of the Furens is to-day the greatest of the works of this sort, at least so far as my knowledge goes, because that of Puentes, on account of a great mistake made in the foundations, was partly destroyed in 1802, and has not since been rebuilt.

The Furens wall reflects the greatest honor on Messrs. Græff, Delocre and Montgolfier, the engineers, who prepared the plans and carried the undertaking through to a successful termination.

If I compare my profile type with the Furens wall, I find to the disadvantage of the former an excess of volume of about 10 per cent., which is certainly to be considered.

I might say that the designers of the reservoir wall profited skillfully by the narrowness of the valley to build on a curve and to narrow the base of their foundations.

They might even have made greater reductions had they taken full advantage of these facilities of which the profile type makes no account. All this is correct; but it is not the essential cause of the difference in question. It arises mainly from their having taken the weight of the masonry at 2,000 kilograms per cubic metre (3,400 pounds per cubic yard), whereas I have taken it at 2,300 kilograms (3,900 pounds). What I saw at the Ternay dam, when as chief engineer I directed its construction, leads me to think that the actual weight of granite masonry, the joints being well filled with mortar and spauls, is not less than 2,300 kilograms (3,900 pounds). The consequences of this difference are easily seen.

This change alone increases the weight of the wall 15 per cent. Where there was before a pressure of 6 kilograms per square centimetre (85 pounds per square inch), we must now count on 6 × 1.15 or 6.90 kilograms (98 pounds).

Having resolved, for the reasons before given, not to exceed the limit of 6 kilograms (85 pounds), I have had to widen the base of the wall. From this arises the difference of 10 per cent. which exists between the given section of my profile and that of the Furens wall.

But having assumed this limit of 6 kilograms (85 pounds) we see that the profile-types can scarcely be reduced—in other words, that they are sufficiently economical.

*Various details.*—It is not uninteresting to examine how the crown of the walls should be built. I have given before the conditions which govern its height and width. I add that the shock of waves, and the occasional presence of ice, should cause all mouldings, steps, projections or hollows at the top of the crown to be suppressed. The parapet itself should, in my opinion, be formed only of a solid wall smoothly rounded at the top.

The ornamentation of the wall of a high dam is only possible on the down-stream side and offers a few difficulties. I think that it must be limited to a sort of inverted festoons, supporting an open work parapet either on cut-stone corbels or on brick ogives. This is the only system of decoration which, in my opinion, suits such works. I have given in figures 12, 15, 18, three specimens for various heights.

It seems proper to place, on the face next the water, iron ladders, by means of which persons who happen to fall into the water can climb out along the wall. Rings should also be put in, to which the service boats can be made fast.

On the down-stream face, cut-stone corbels, arranged in quincunx order, will allow small scaffolds to be placed, and, if necessary, the face of the wall can be visited and repaired.

---

### GENERAL OBSERVATIONS.

At the beginning of the present note I mentioned cursorily the services which husbanding water may render to agriculture, to manufacturers, and to the health of cities.

I might also add that our inland navigation receives its share of the benefits, sometimes in the supply of water for canals and again in regulating the discharge of rivers.

The essential instrument for this case, which consists in storing up the surplus of the winter's rains for use in summer, is the reservoir.

Placed necessarily in the upper parts of valleys, the reservoir presents no other difficulties nor essential expense than the building of the dam.

Earthen embankments or masonry walls may be used in forming these dams. The wall, however, especially in the South, is to be preferred.

It is certain that when the railway system shall have been finished, attention will be given to navigation and to storing water. Then works of this sort will become as common as to-day they are rare.

Often they will form a good investment for capital, and private industry will be interested in them, in order to sell the stored-up water.

The establishment of a reservoir will almost always be of a generally useful character to which the State cannot be indifferent and which will call for its assistance.

Counties and parishes will often have a more direct interest in these kinds of works, and should contribute to them.

Finally, manufacturers and agriculturists who derive any benefit from the water should be expected to pay for the good they receive.

It is in this way, coming from different sources, that the funds for building reservoirs will be obtained.

So soon as private parties take the matter up, the question of economy necessarily occupies a foremost place. Manufacturers and agriculturists, who cannot obtain their funds by means of the easy way of taxation, are obliged to count with their purse and to pay no more for a service than it is actually worth to them.

This consideration obliges the engineer to study the matter of cost very closely, and to solve it in the best way for all the interests concerned.

A district needs a reservoir of a given capacity, an examination of the sites easily shows the depth of water required to obtain the wished for amount. This depth found, the dimensions and price of the dam are deduced, and consequently the cost of the water stored up.

This is probably the shape in which the problem will generally be presented to the engineer.

But it will also frequently happen that a minimum of volume being fixed, we may wish to know what it would cost to increase this minimum, and at what limit the increase in the volume stored up would cease to be advantageous.

These questions, in order to be properly solved, require the quick preparation of plans. The engineer must study all the combinations which present themselves, promptly and with sufficient exactness.

It was in view of this rapid study that I formerly prepared the present article for my own service. It is still in view of this study that I now offer it to constructors.

## SUMMARY

### OF THE PLATES OF THE TYPES OF RESERVOIR WALLS.

Fig. 1. Profile type of reservoir walls.
" 2. Type for height of 5 metres, 16.40 feet.
" 3. " " 10 " 32.81 "
" 4. " " 15 " 49.21 "
" 5. " " 20 " 65.62 "
" 6. " " 25 " 82.02 "
" 7. " " 30 " 98.43 "
" 8. " " 35 " 114.83 "
" 9. " " 40 " 131.24 "
" 10. " " 45 " 147.64 "
" 11. " " 50 " 164.04 "

Figs. 12, 13, 14. Type of crown applicable to walls up to 15 metres (49.21 feet) in height.

*Elevation.—Cross section.—Wall* 10 metres (32.81 feet) *in height seen from down stream.*

## SUMMARY.

Figs. 15, 16, 17. Type of crown applicable to walls from 15 to 30 metres (49.21 to 98.43 feet) in height.

*Elevation.—Cross section.—Wall* 25 metres (82.02 feet) *in height, seen from down stream.*

Figs. 18, 19, 20. Type of crown applicable to walls from 30 to 50 metres (98.43 to 164.04 feet) in height.

*Elevation.—Cross section.—Wall* 40 metres (131.24 feet) *in height, seen from down stream.*

Fig. 21. Graphic comparison of the profile type with the Furens Dam, (France).

Fig. 22. Graphic comparison of the profile type with the Puentes Dam, (Spain).

Fig. 23. Graphic comparison of the profile type with the Val de Infierno Dam, (Spain).

Fig. 24. Graphic comparison of the profile type with the Rio Lozoya Dam, (Spain).

Fig. 25. Graphic comparison of the profile type with the Alicante Dam, (Spain).

Fig. 26. Graphic comparison of the profile type with the Ternay Dam, (France).

Fig. 27. Graphic comparison of the profile type with the Habra Dam, (Algiers).

Fig. 28. Graphic comparison of the profile type with the Nijar Dam, (Spain).

Fig. 29. Graphic comparison of the profile type with the Elcho Dam, (Spain).

Fig. 30. Graphic comparison of the profile type with the Grosbois Dam, (France).

Fig. 31. Graphic comparison of the profile type with the Bosméléa Dam, (France).

Fig. 32. Graphic comparison of the profile type with the Lampy Dam, (France).

Fig. 33. Graphic comparison of the profile type with the Glomel Dam, (France).

Fig. 34. Graphic comparison of the profile type with the Vioreau Dam, (France).

---

In figures 21 to 34 inclusive the parts shaded thus  belong to the profile types; those shaded thus  belong to the structure given, but are outside of the profile type; those not shaded are common to both.

## TABLE Ia.

### GIVING IN FEET THE PRINCIPAL DIMENSIONS OF RESERVOIR WALLS.

| Depth of the water. | Height of the first step. | Width on top. | Height of top above the water. | VERSED SINE. | | BÂTIR OF PEDESTAL. | | RADIUS OF CURVATURE. | | Total width of the base. |
|---|---|---|---|---|---|---|---|---|---|---|
| | | | | Up-stream. | Down-stream. | Up-stream. | Down-stream. | Up-stream. | Down-stream. | |
| H | H' | AB | BC | DN | LM | GF | IK | R | R' | IF |
| feet. | feet. | feet. | feet. | feet. | feet. | feet. | feet. | feet. | feet. | feet. |
| 16.40 | | 6.56 | 1.64 | 3.28 | 3.28 | | | 42.65 | 42.65 | 13.12 |
| 32.81 | | 8.20 | 3.28 | 6.56 | 8.20 | | | 85.30 | 69.72 | 22.96 |
| 49.21 | | 9.84 | 4.92 | 9.84 | 14.76 | | | 127.96 | 89.41 | 34.44 |
| 65.62 | | 11.48 | 6.56 | 13.12 | 22.97 | | | 170.61 | 105.22 | 47.57 |
| 82.02 | | 13.12 | 8.20 | 16.40 | 32.81 | | | 213.26 | 118.94 | 62.34 |
| 98.43 | | 14.76 | 9.84 | 19.69 | 44.29 | | | 255.91 | 131.37 | 78.75 |
| 114.83 | | 16.40 | 11.48 | 22.97 | 57.42 | | | 298.56 | 143.54 | 96.79 |
| 131.24 | 16.40 | 16.40 | 11.48 | 22.97 | 57.42 | | | 298.56 | 143.54 | 130.69 |
| 147.64 | 32.81 | 16.40 | 11.48 | 22.97 | 57.42 | 10.94 | 16.40 | 298.56 | 143.54 | 158.04 |
| 164.04 | 49.21 | 16.40 | 11.48 | 22.97 | 57.42 | 21.87 | 32.81 | 298.56 | 143.54 | 185.38 |
| | | | | | | 32.81 | 49.21 | | | |

## TABLE Ib.

### GIVING IN METRES THE PRINCIPAL DIMENSIONS OF RESERVOIR WALLS.

| Depth of the water. | Height of the first step. | Width on top. | Height of top above the water. | VERSED SINE. | | BÂTIR OF PEDESTAL. | | RADIUS OF CURVATURE. | | Total width of the base. |
|---|---|---|---|---|---|---|---|---|---|---|
| | | | | Up-stream. | Down-stream. | Up-stream. | Down-stream. | Up-stream. | Down-stream. | |
| H | H' | AB | BC | DN | LM | GF | IK | R | R' | IF |
| metres. | metres. | metres. | metres. | metres. | metres. | metres. | metres. | metres. | metres. | metres. |
| 5.00 | | 2.00 | 0.50 | 1.00 | 1.00 | | | 13.00 | 13.00 | 4.00 |
| 10.00 | | 2.50 | 1.00 | 2.00 | 2.50 | | | 26.00 | 21.25 | 7.00 |
| 15.00 | | 3.00 | 1.50 | 3.00 | 4.50 | | | 39.00 | 27.25 | 10.50 |
| 20.00 | | 3.50 | 2.00 | 4.00 | 7.00 | | | 52.00 | 32.07 | 14.50 |
| 25.00 | | 4.00 | 2.50 | 5.00 | 10.00 | | | 65.00 | 36.25 | 19.00 |
| 30.00 | | 4.50 | 3.00 | 6.00 | 13.50 | | | 78.00 | 40.08 | 24.00 |
| 35.00 | | 5.00 | 3.50 | 7.00 | 17.50 | | | 91.00 | 43.75 | 29.50 |
| 40.00 | 5.00 | 5.00 | 3.50 | 7.00 | 17.50 | | | 91.00 | 43.75 | 39.83 |
| 45.00 | 10.00 | 5.00 | 3.50 | 7.00 | 17.50 | 3.33 | 5.00 | 91.00 | 43.75 | 48.17 |
| 50.00 | 15.00 | 5.00 | 3.50 | 7.00 | 17.50 | 6.67 | 10.00 | 91.00 | 43.75 | 56.50 |
| | | | | | | 10.00 | 15.00 | | | |

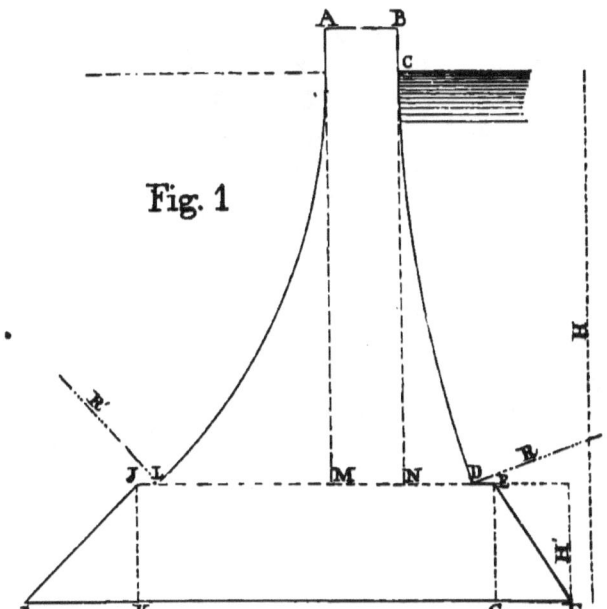

Fig. 1

STUDY ON RESERVOIR WALLS. 53

### TABLE IIa.

### SHOWING THE PRINCIPAL QUANTITIES IN THE VARIOUS PROFILE TYPES FOR ONE FOOT IN LENGTH OF THE WALL.

| QUANTITIES. | 1ST TYPE. Fig. 2. | 2D TYPE. Fig. 3. | 3D TYPE. Fig. 4. | 4TH TYPE. Fig. 5. | 5TH TYPE. Fig. 6. | 6TH TYPE. Fig. 7. | 7TH TYPE. Fig. 8. | 8TH TYPE. Fig. 9. | 9TH TYPE. Fig. 10. | 10TH TYPE. Fig. 11. |
|---|---|---|---|---|---|---|---|---|---|---|
| Depth of water = $H$ .............feet | 16.40 | 32.81 | 49.21 | 65.62 | 82.02 | 98.43 | 114.83 | 131.24 | 147.64 | 164.04 |
| Horizontal component of pressure = $ED$.tons | 4.20 | 16.80 | 37.80 | 67.20 | 105.00 | 151.19 | 205.79 | 268.79 | 340.19 | 419.88 |
| Vertical component of pressure = ....tons | 1.18 | 4.52 | 10.16 | 18.06 | 28.22 | 40.65 | 55.31 | 109.03 | 156.72 | 209.87 |
| Resultant = $AB$.tons | 4.35 | 1.74 | 39.15 | 69.58 | 108.72 | 156.55 | 213.10 | 290.06 | 374.55 | 469.50 |
| Angle of resultant with the horizon. | 15° 2′ 41″ | 15° 2′ 41″ | 15° 2′ 41″ | 15° 2′ 41″ | 15° 2′ 41″ | 15° 2′ 41″ | 15° 2′ 41″ | 22° 4′ 45″ | 24° 44′ 3″ | 26° 33′ 6″ |
| Volume of masonry in the wall .....cub. yds. | 5.65 | 16.69 | 34.05 | 58.42 | 90.65 | 131.51 | 180.92 | 251.47 | 337.52 | 442.03 |
| Weight of the wall................tons | 11.04 | 32.60 | 66.43 | 114.11 | 177.06 | 256.47 | 353.38 | 491.19 | 661.22 | 863.41 |
| Thickness of the wall at the base......feet | 13.12 | 22.96 | 34.44 | 47.57 | 62.34 | 78.74 | 96.79 | 130.69 | 158.04 | 185.38 |
| Sum of the weights and vertical pressures ................$CD$.tons | 12.16 | 37.12 | 76.59 | 132.17 | 205.30 | 297.11 | 406.70 | 600.22 | 817.93 | 1073.28 |
| Pressure on the base per square { maximum.lbs | 11.59 | 22.05 | 33.49 | 45.08 | 57.24 | 69.25 | 81.40 | 74.48 | 78.57 | 84.37 |
| inch, reservoir empty.... { mean...lbs | 11.59 | 19.64 | 26.57 | 33.07 | 39.15 | 44.94 | 50.45 | 51.86 | 57.80 | 63.40 |
| Pressure on the base per { maximum.lbs | 20.49 | 42.40 | 57.66 | 67.83 | 73.63 | 77.02 | 77.59 | 71.23 | 75.75 | 80.69 |
| square inch, reservoir full { mean...lbs | 12.86 | 22.33 | 30.67 | 38.30 | 45.51 | 52.01 | 58.22 | 63.45 | 71.37 | 79.85 |
| Overturning moment, lever arm of 1 foot.tons | 75.51 | 602.15 | 2034.28 | 4824.41 | 9413.21 | 16674.23 | 25850.28 | 38566.32 | 54925.54 | 75358.75 |
| Moment of stability, lever arm of 1 foot.tons | 281.51 | 1582.04 | 5094.59 | 12530.80 | 26028.83 | 48546.79 | 83539.52 | 161902.99 | 262860.68 | 400642.83 |
| Ratio of the first to the second......... | 0.27 | 0.38 | 0.40 | 0.39 | 0.36 | 0.34 | 0.31 | 0.24 | 0.21 | 0.19 |
| Ratio of the horizontal to the vertical pressures................... | 0.35 | 0.45 | 0.49 | 0.51 | 0.51 | 0.51 | 0.50 | 0.45 | 0.42 | 0.39 |
| Mean thickness or ratio of the volume of masonry to the depth $H$ ......cub. yds | 0.34 | 0.51 | 0.69 | 0.89 | 1.105 | 1.35 | 1.58 | 1.92 | 2.28 | 2.69 |

## TABLE IIb.

### SHOWING IN METRIC DENOMINATIONS THE PRINCIPAL QUANTITIES IN THE VARIOUS PROFILE TYPES FOR ONE METRE IN LENGTH OF THE WALL.

| QUANTITIES. | 1ST TYPE. Fig. 2. | 2D TYPE. Fig. 3. | 3D TYPE. Fig. 4. | 4TH TYPE. Fig. 5. | 5TH TYPE. Fig. 6. | 6TH TYPE. Fig. 7. | 7TH TYPE. Fig. 8. | 8TH TYPE. Fig. 9. | 9TH TYPE. Fig. 10. | 10TH TYPE. Fig. 11. |
|---|---|---|---|---|---|---|---|---|---|---|
| Depth of water = $H$ .............. *metres* | 5.00 | 10.00 | 15.00 | 20.00 | 25.00 | 30.00 | 35.00 | 40.00 | 45.00 | 50.00 |
| Horizontal component of pressure = $ED$ ........... *m. tons* | 12.500 | 50.000 | 112.50 | 200.00 | 312.50 | 450.00 | 612.50 | 800.00 | 1012.50 | 1250.00 |
| Vertical component of pressure .... *m. tons* | 3.356 | 13.439 | 30.239 | 53.758 | 83.996 | 120.955 | 164.633 | 324.508 | 466.433 | 624.633 |
| Resultant = $AB$ ............ *m. tons* | 12.944 | 51.775 | 116.493 | 207.099 | 323.592 | 465.972 | 634.240 | 863.311 | 1114.770 | 1397.380 |
| Angle of resultant with the horizon. | 15° 2′ 41″ | 15° 2′ 41″ | 15° 2′ 41″ | 15° 2′ 41″ | 15° 2′ 41″ | 15° 2′ 41″ | 15° 2′ 41″ | 22° 4′ 45″ | 24° 44′ 3″ | 26° 33′ 6″ |
| Volume of masonry in the wall .... *cub. met.* | 14.28 | 42.19 | 85.96 | 147.66 | 229.12 | 331.89 | 457.29 | 635.62 | 835.64 | 1117.29 |
| Weight of the wall ............ *m. tons* | 32.844 | 97.027 | 197.708 | 339.618 | 526.976 | 763.347 | 1051.774 | 1461.921 | 1997.979 | 2569.774 |
| Thickness of the wall at the base .. *metres* | 4.00 | 7.00 | 10.50 | 14.50 | 19.00 | 24.00 | 29.50 | 39.83 | 48.17 | 56.50 |
| Sum of the weights and vertical pressures = $CD$ ........... *m. tons* | 36.204 | 110.466 | 227.947 | 393.376 | 610.972 | 884.302 | 1216.407 | 1786.429 | 2434.412 | 3194.407 |
| Pressure on the base per square centimetre, reservoir empty } max. *kilos.* | 0.82 | 1.56 | 2.37 | 3.19 | 4.05 | 4.90 | 5.76 | 5.27 | 5.56 | 5.97 |
|  mean *kilos.* | 0.82 | 1.39 | 1.88 | 2.34 | 2.77 | 3.18 | 3.57 | 3.67 | 4.99 | 4.55 |
| Pressure on the base per square centimetre, reservoir full } max. *kilos.* | 1.45 | 3.00 | 4.08 | 4.80 | 5.21 | 5.45 | 5.49 | 5.04 | 5.36 | 5.71 |
|  mean *kilos.* | 0.91 | 1.58 | 2.17 | 2.71 | 3.22 | 3.68 | 4.12 | 4.49 | 5.05 | 5.65 |
| Overturning moment, lever arm of 1 metre ............ *m. tons* | 20.88 | 166.50 | 562.50 | 1334.00 | 2603.13 | 4500.00 | 7147.88 | 10664.00 | 15187.50 | 20837.50 |
| Moment of stability, lever arm of 1 metre ........... *m. tons* | 77.84 | 437.45 | 1468.71 | 3453.84 | 7197.25 | 13443.70 | 23099.57 | 44767.91 | 72667.20 | 110982.03 |
| Ratio of the first to the second .......... | 0.27 | 0.38 | 0.40 | 0.39 | 0.36 | 0.34 | 0.31 | 0.24 | 0.21 | 0.19 |
| Ratio of the horizontal to the vertical pressures .................... | 0.35 | 0.44 | 0.49 | 0.50 | 0.51 | 0.50 | 0.50 | 0.44 | 0.41 | 0.39 |
| Mean thickness or ratio of the volume of masonry to the depth $H$..... *cub. met.* | 2.86 | 4.22 | 5.73 | 7.38 | 9.16 | 11.06 | 13.07 | 15.89 | 19.01 | 22.35 |

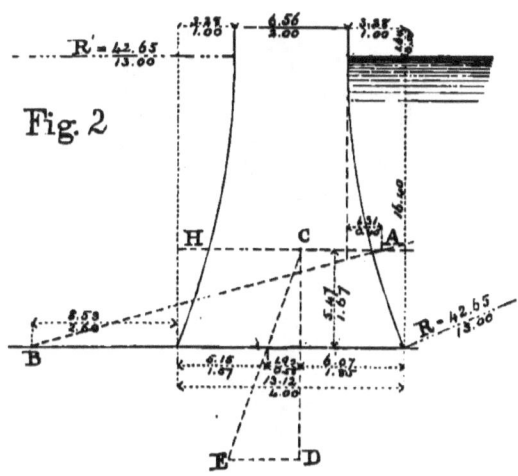

Fig. 2

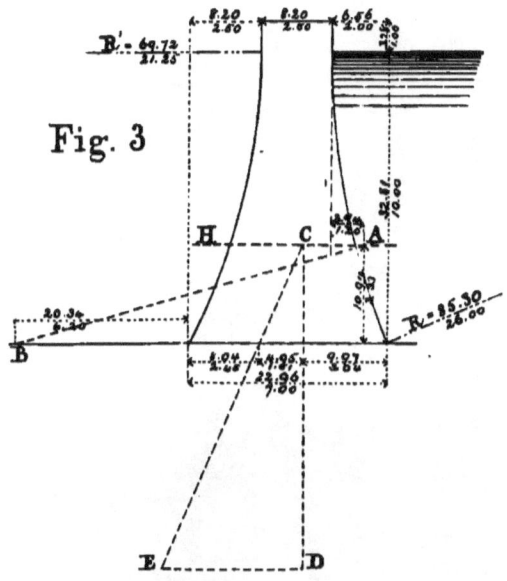

Fig. 3

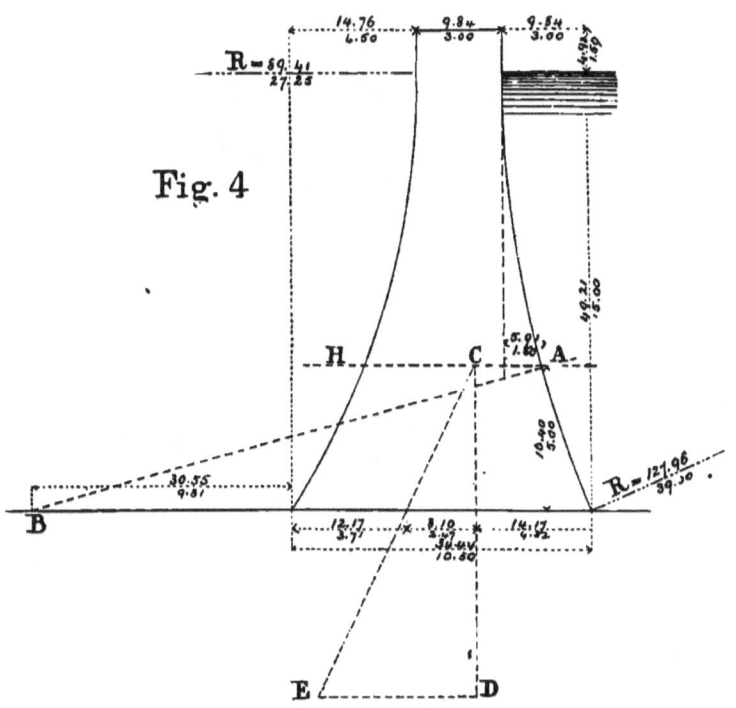

Fig. 4

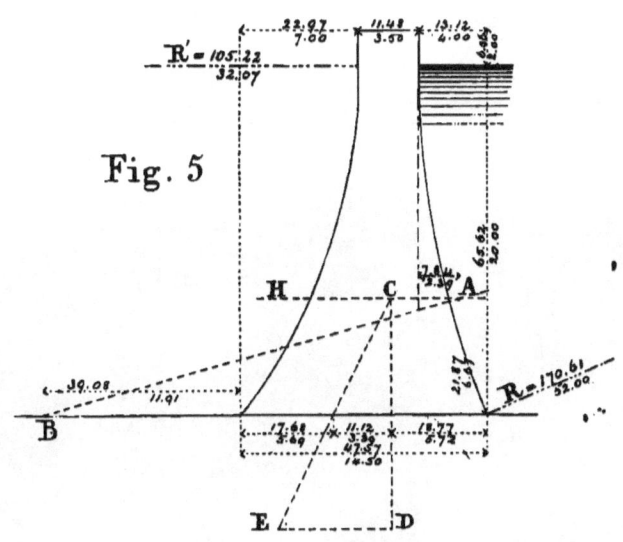

Fig. 5

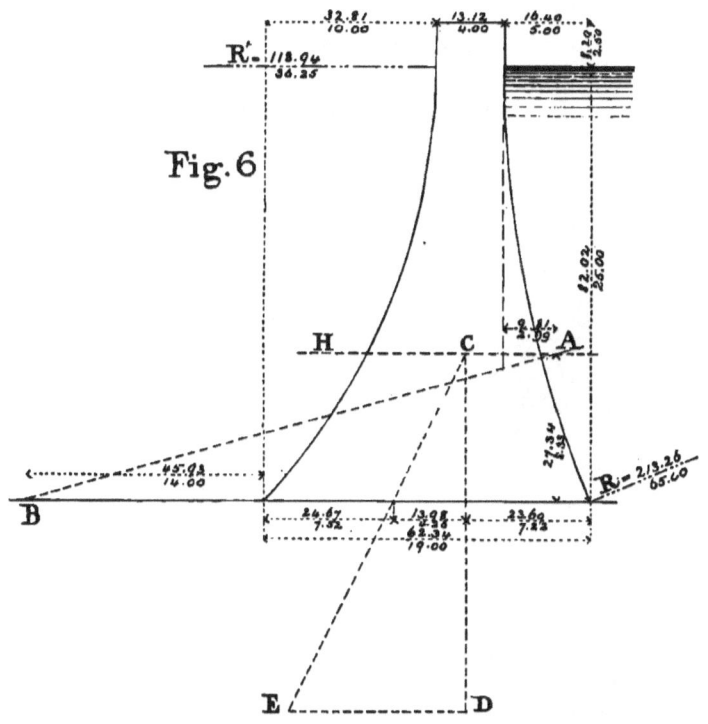

Fig. 6

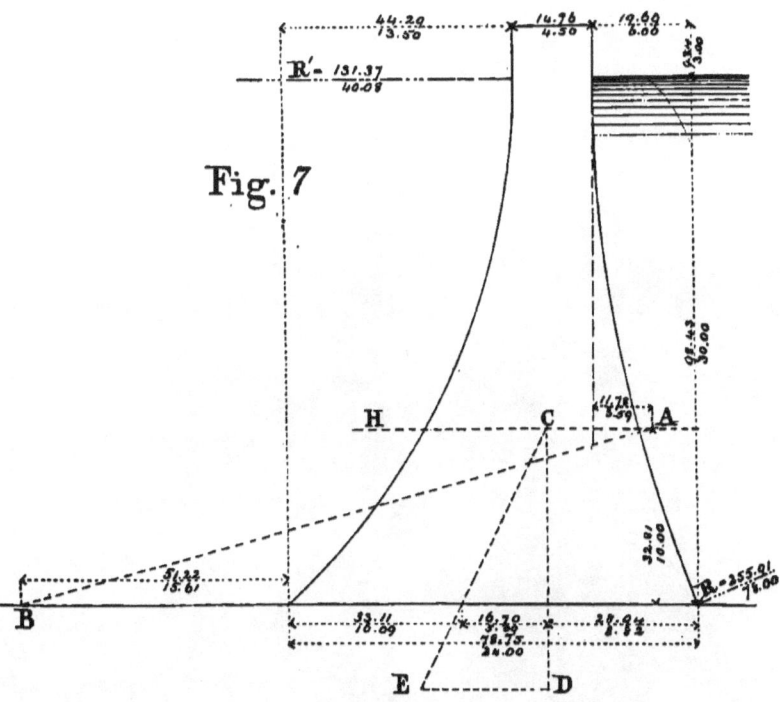

Fig. 7

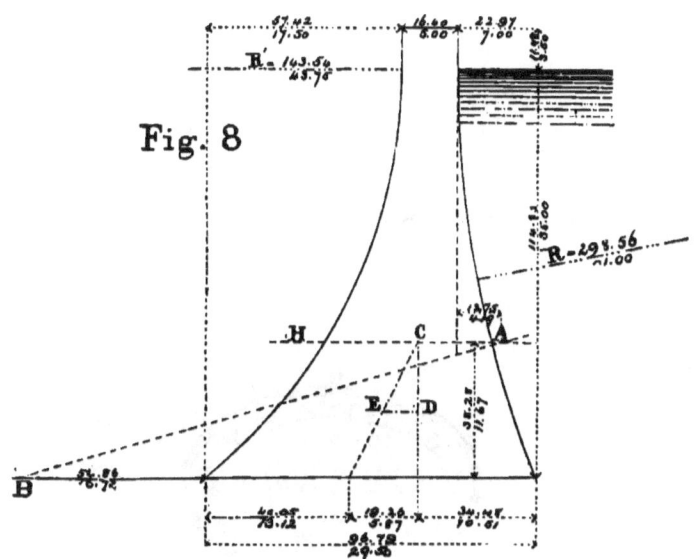

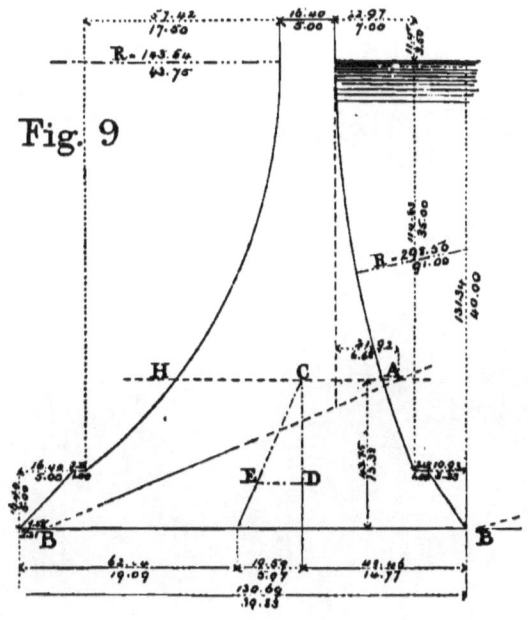

57.42
17.50
16.40
5.00
22.97
7.00
H
C
A
E
D
B


Fig. 10

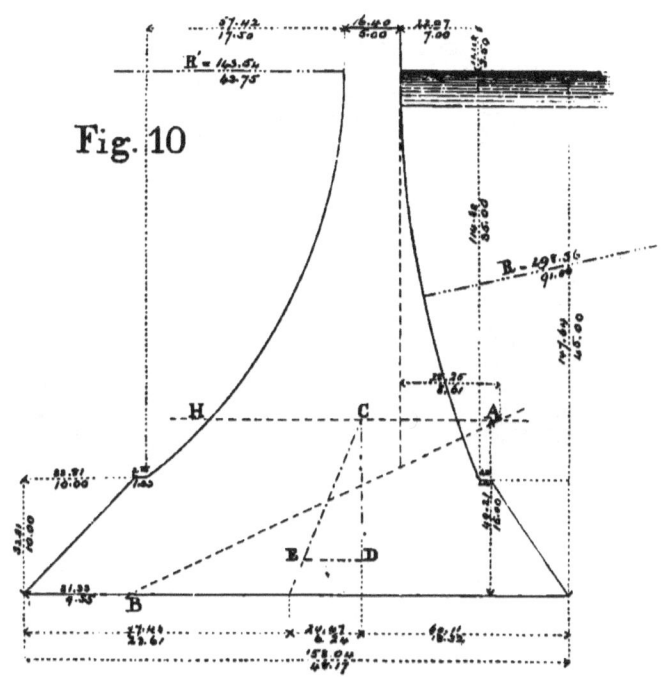

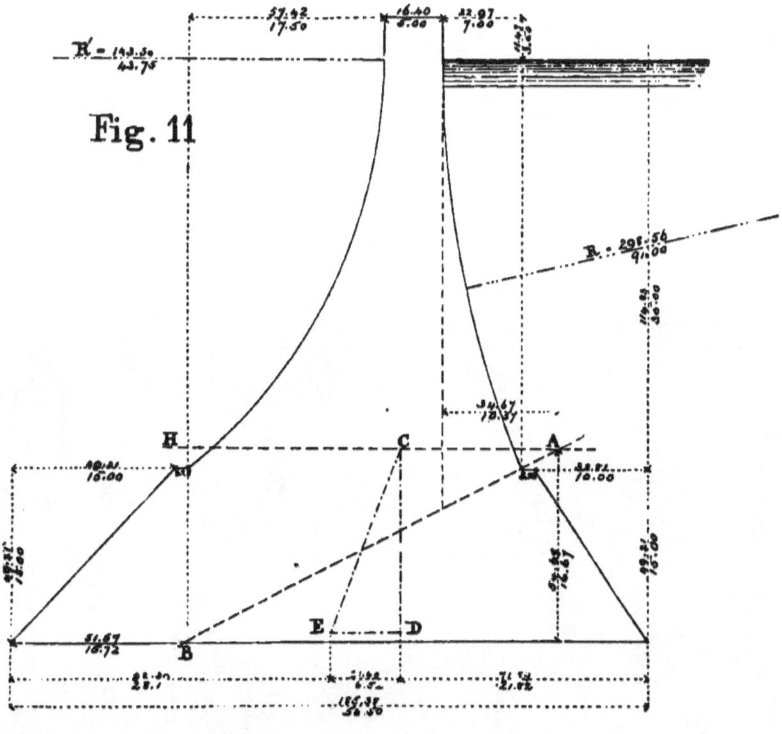

57.42
17.50
16.40
5.00
22.97
7.00
R = 298.56
H
C
A
E
D
B


Fig. 11

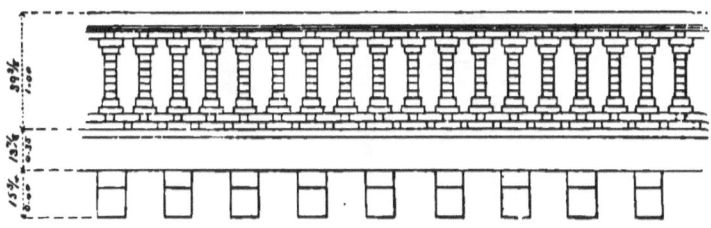

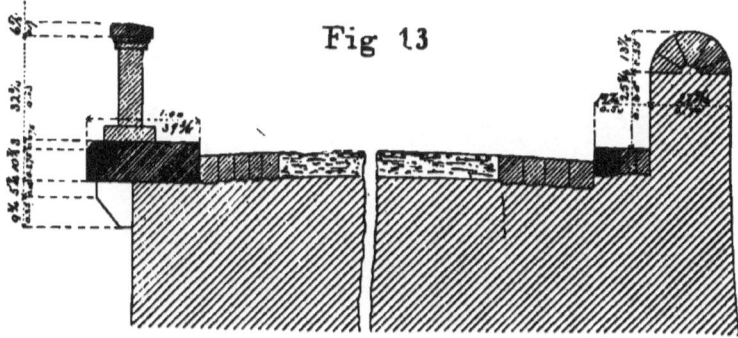

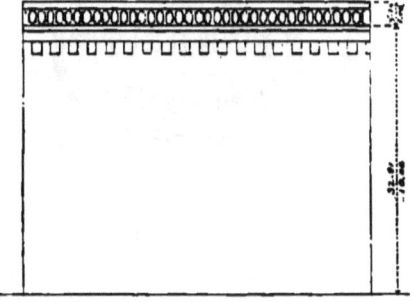

Fig 14

Fig 15

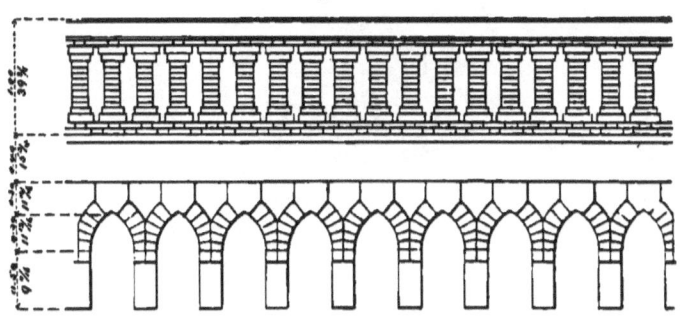

Fig 16

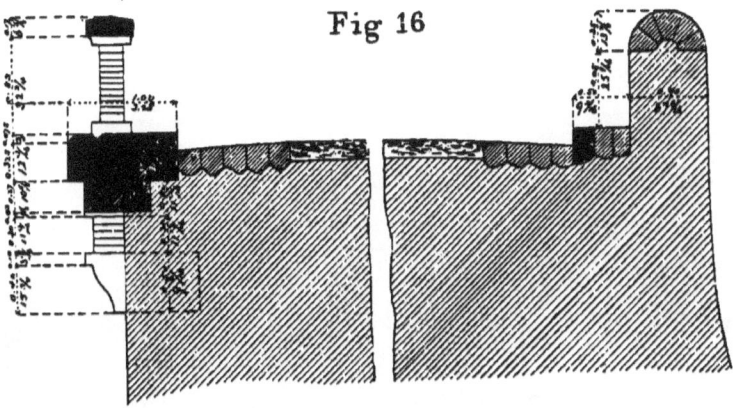

## Fig 17

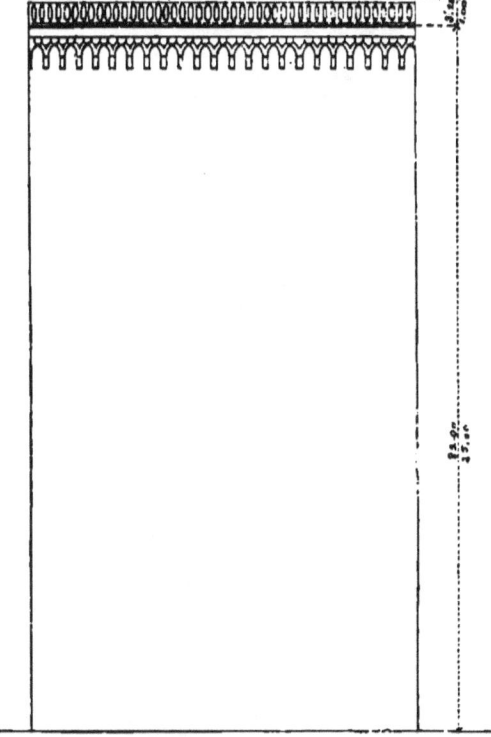

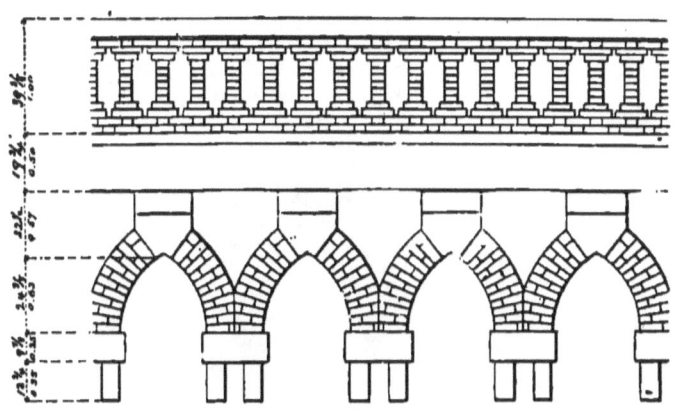

Fig 18

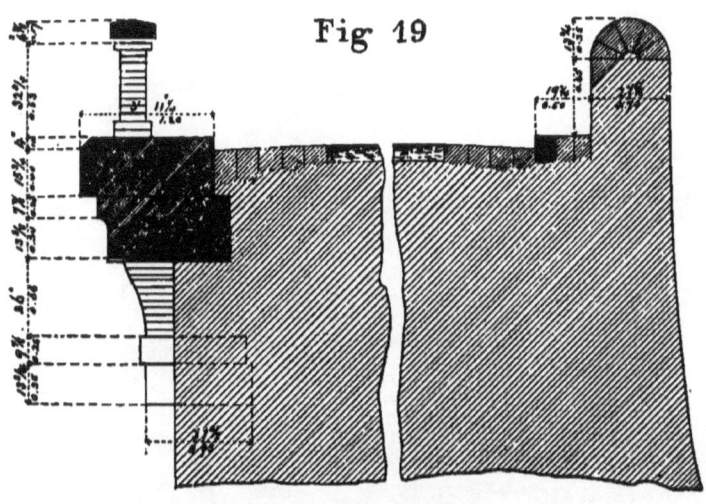

Fig 19

Fig 20

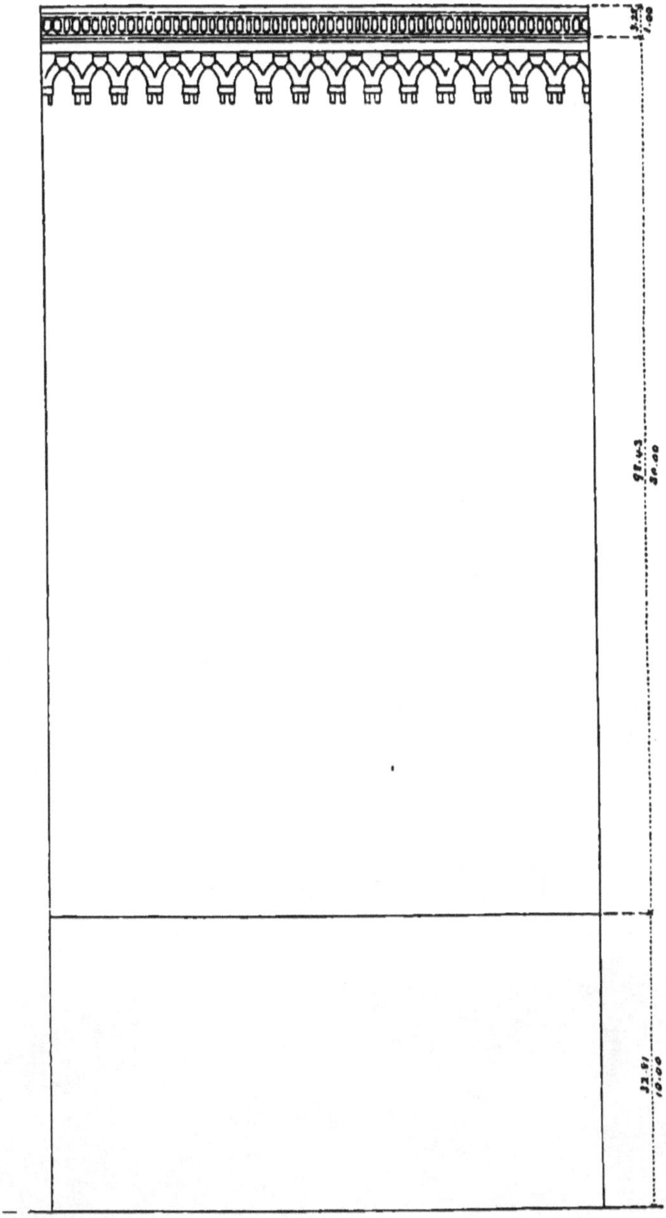

Fig 21

*Graphic comparison of the Profile Type with the profile of*

Furens Dam, (France)

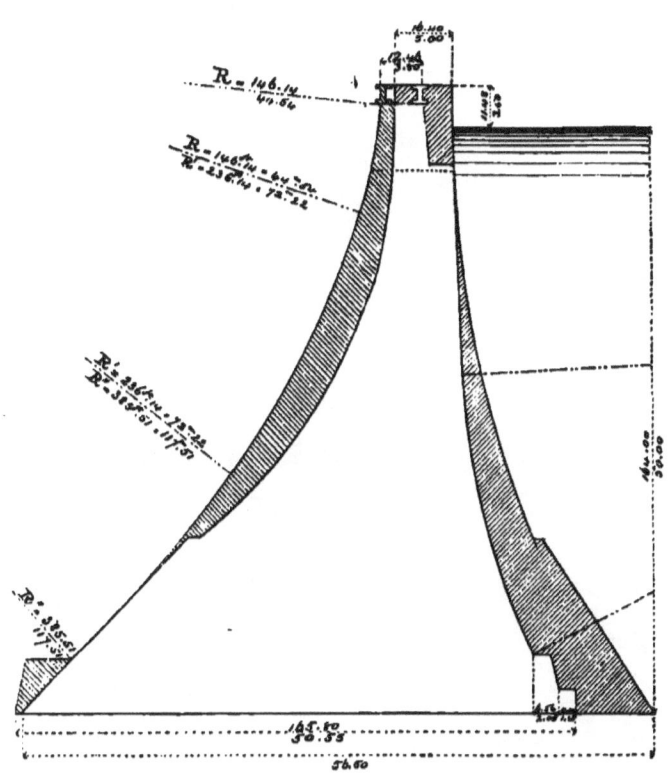

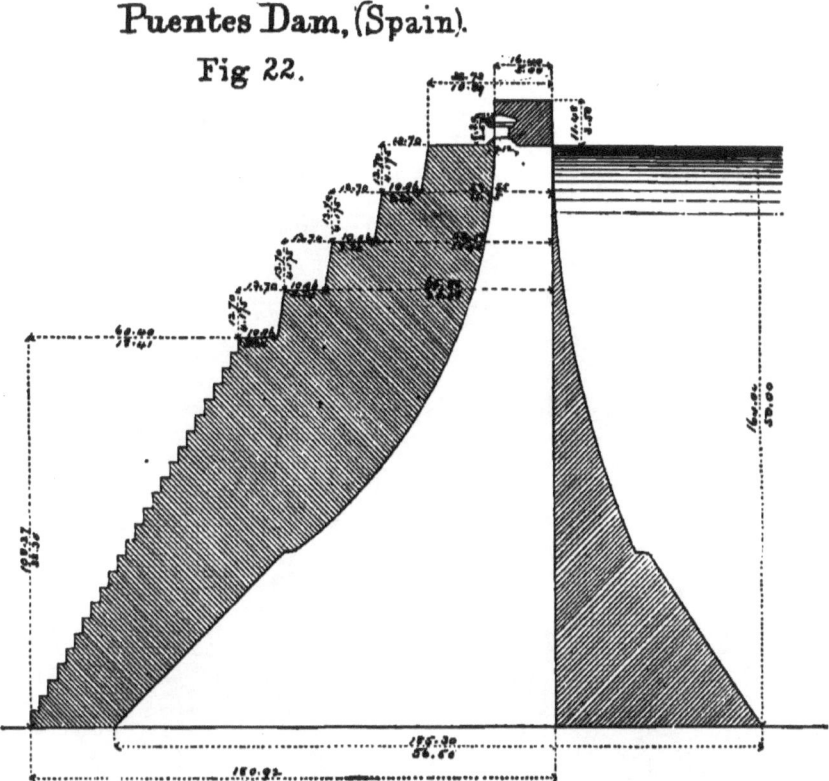

Puentes Dam, (Spain).
Fig 22.

# Fig 23

*Graphic comparison of the Profile Type with the profile of the*

## Val del Infierno Dam, (Spain)

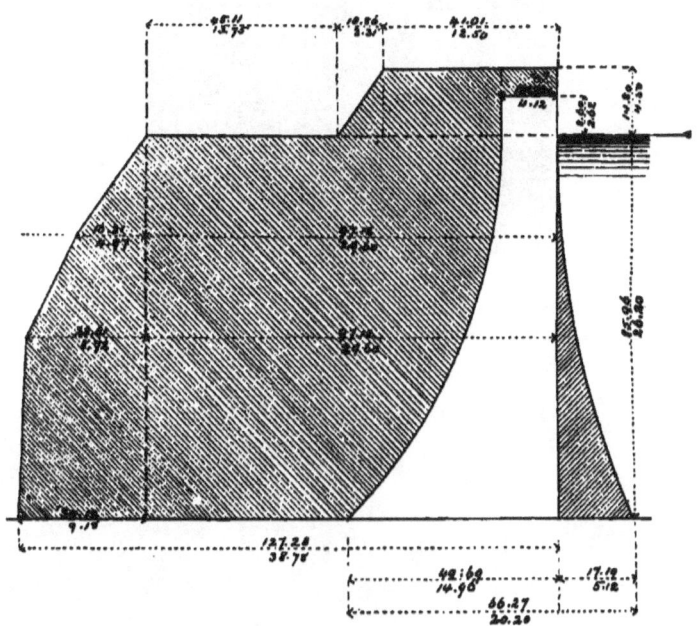

### Fig 24.

*Graphic comparison of the Profile Type with the profile of the*
Rio Lozoya Dam, (Spain)

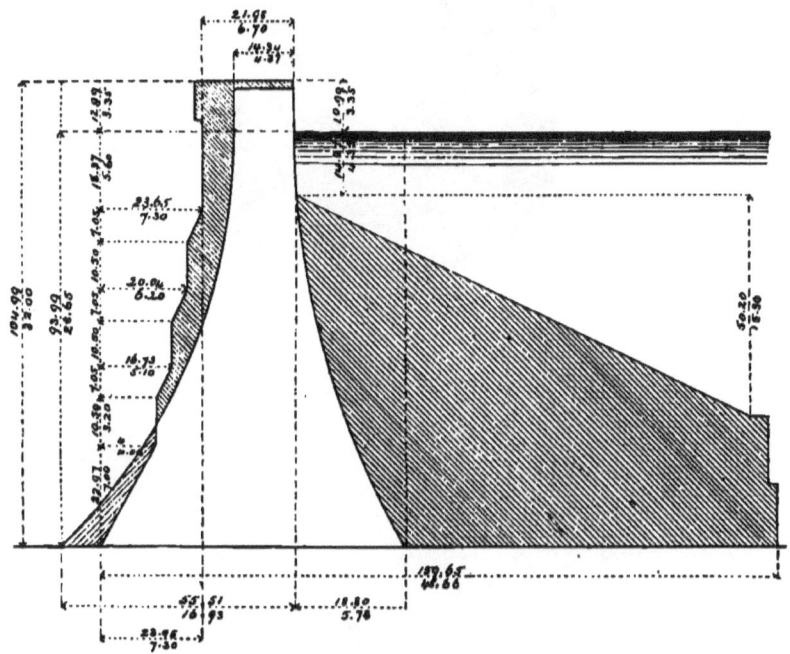

## Fig 25

*Graphic comparison of the Profile Type with the profile of the*
## Alicante Dam, (Spain)

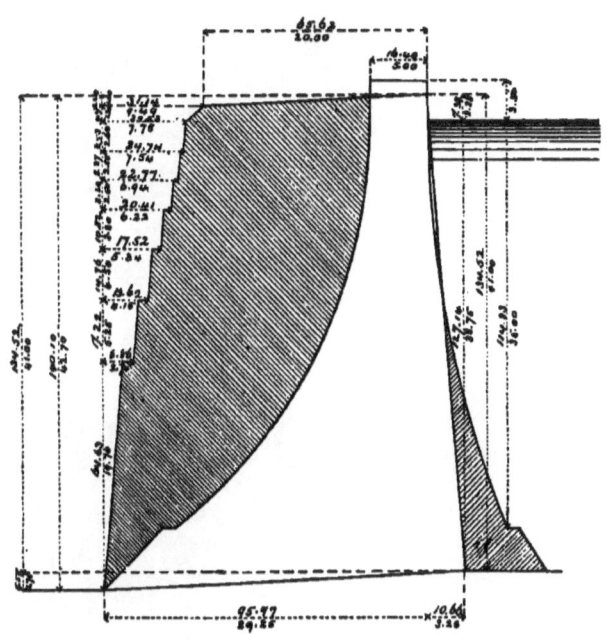

## Fig 26

*Graphic comparison of the Profile Type with the profile of the*
Ternay Dam, (France)

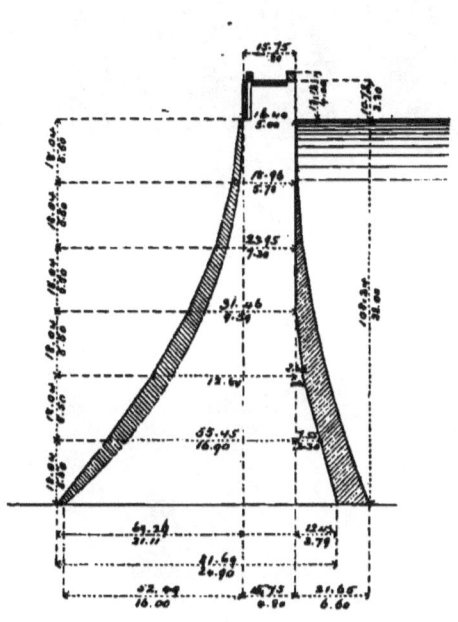

### Fig 27

*Graphic comparison of the Profile Type with the profile of the*
Habra Dam, (Algiers)

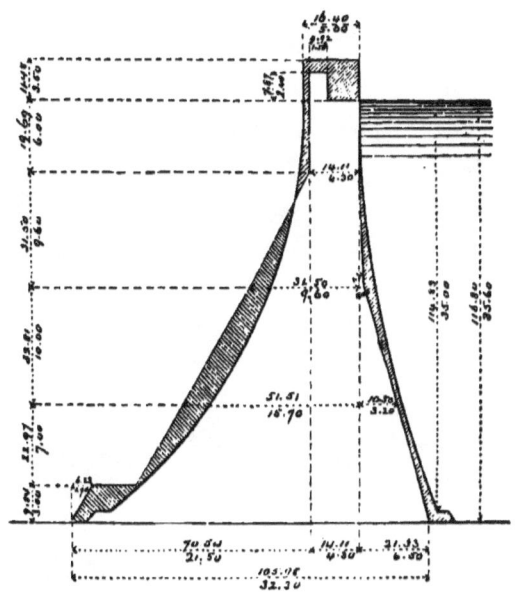

### Fig 28

*Graphic comparison of the Profile Type with the profile of the*
## Nijar Dam, (Spain)

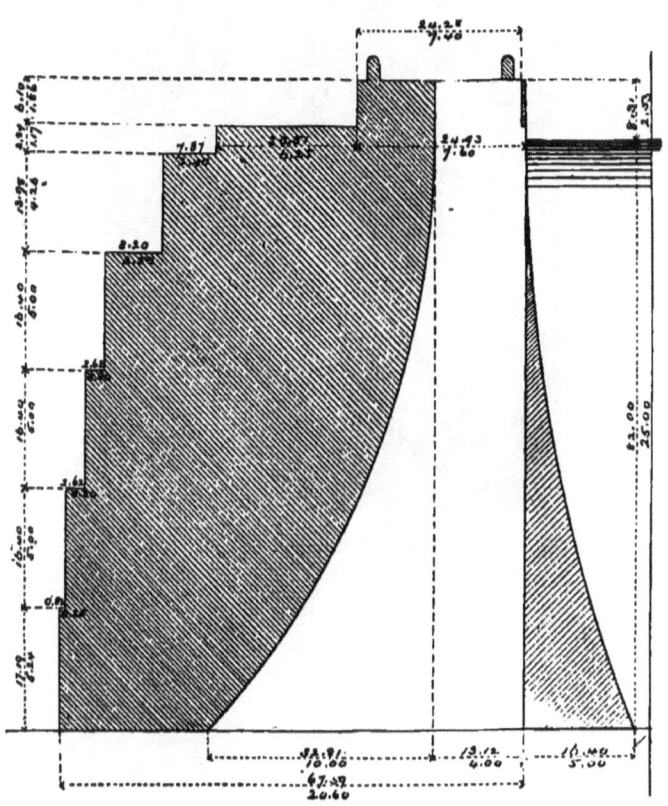

### Fig 29

*Graphic comparison of the Profile Type with the profile of the*
### Elcho Dam, (Spain)

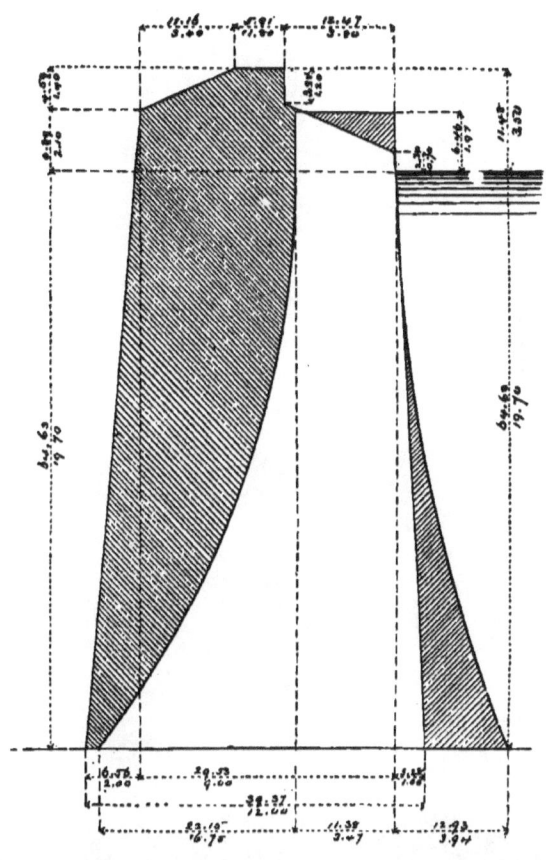

### Fig 30
*Graphic comparison of the Profile Type with the profile of the*
### Gros-Bois Dam, (France)

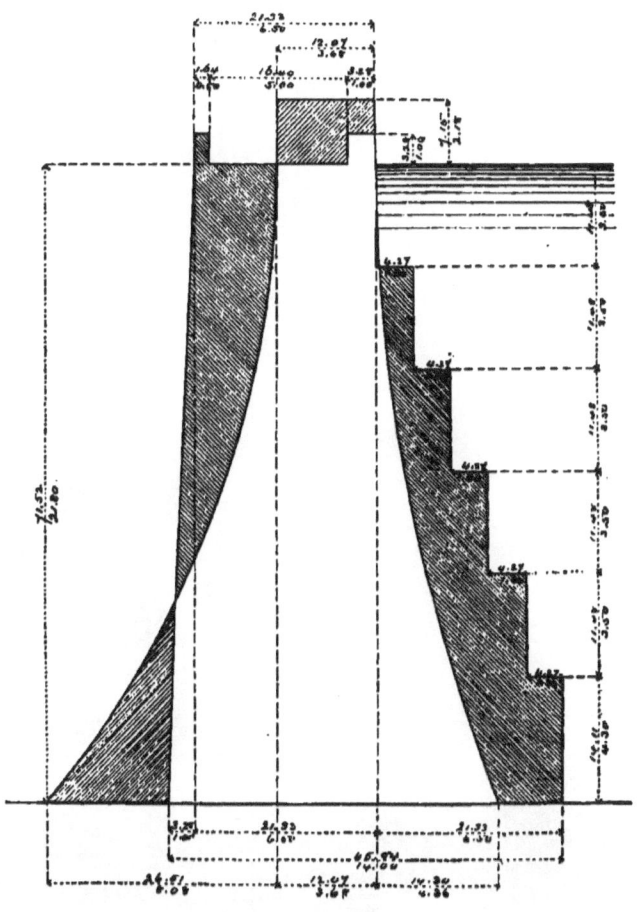

### Fig 31

*Graphic comparison of the Profile Type with the profile of the*
Bosmélea Dam, (France)

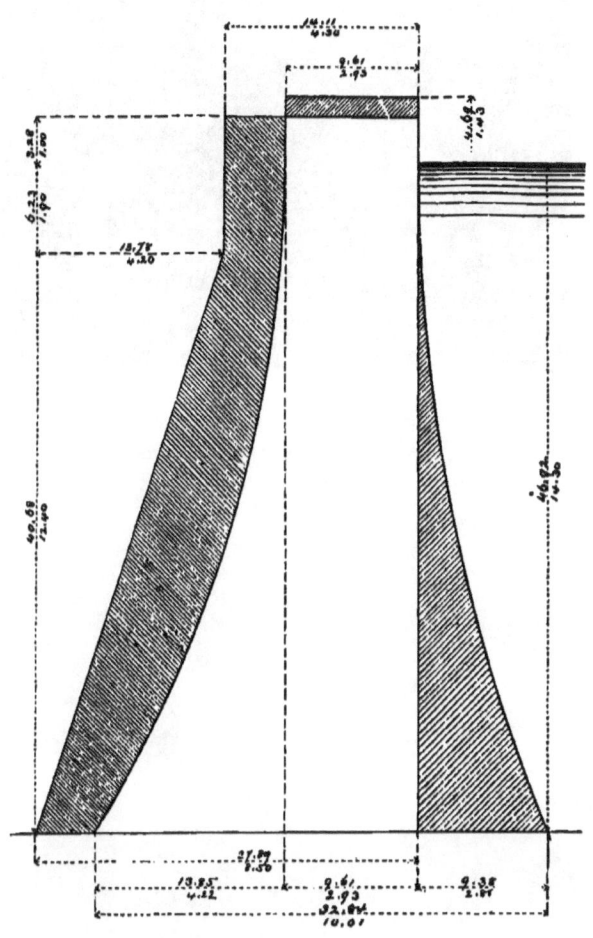

## Fig 32

*Graphic comparison of the Profile Type with the profile of the*
## Lampy Dam, (France)

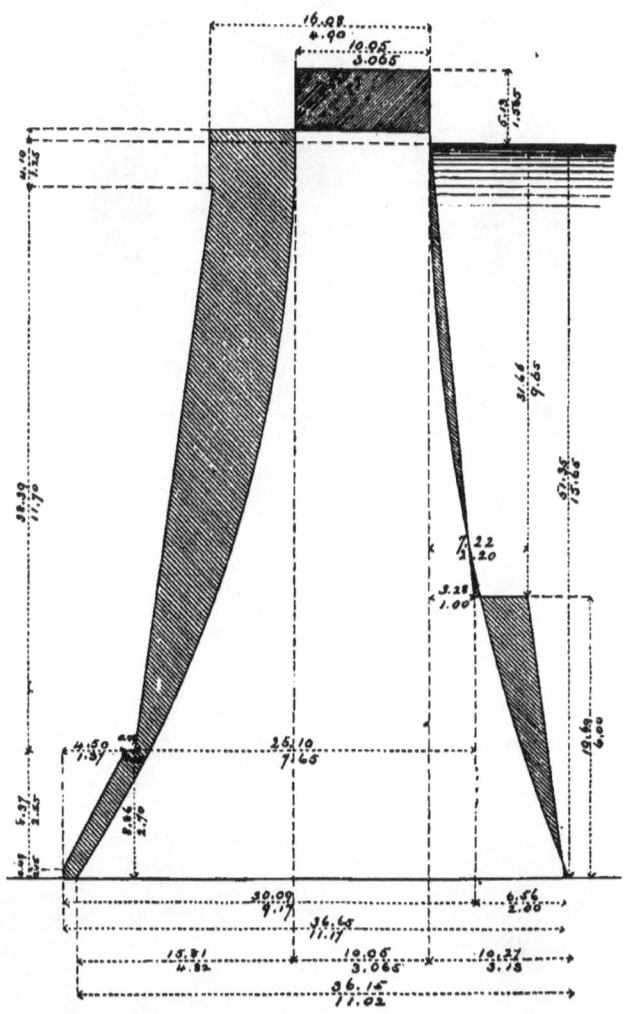

**Fig 33**

*Graphic comparison of the Profile Type with the profile of the*
**Glomel Dam, (France)**

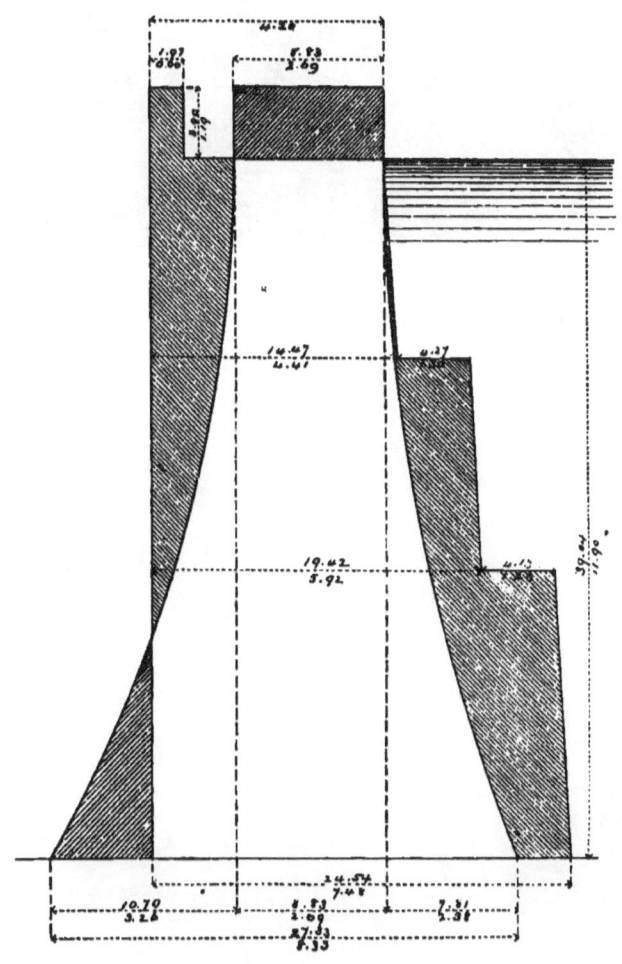

## Fig 34

*Graphic comparison of the Profile Type with the profile of the*
### Vioreau Dam, (France)

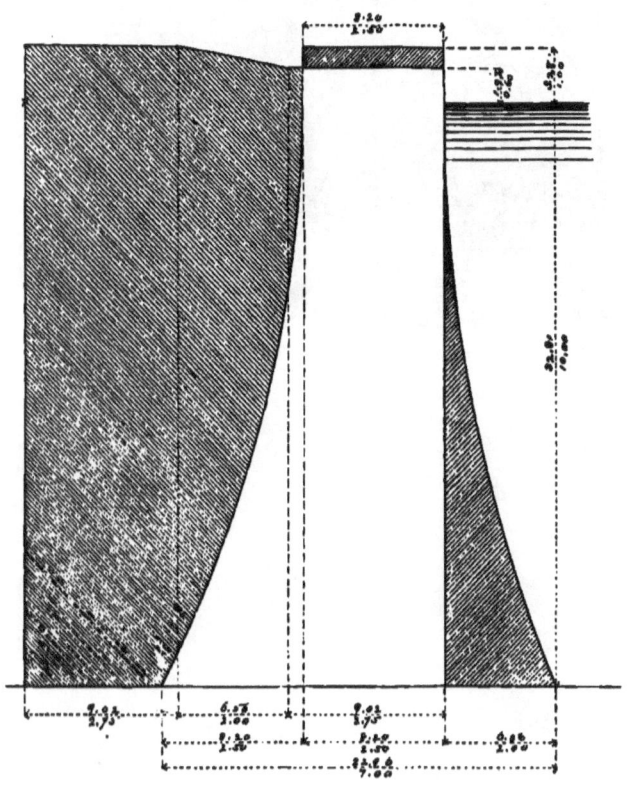

www.ingramcontent.com/pod-product-compliance
Lightning Source LLC
Chambersburg PA
CBHW030409170426
43202CB00010B/1541